Dedication

I dedicate this book to all of those who have suffered and died at the hands of those who practice racism and discrimination.

To all of those courageous people who strive daily to eradicate racism by protesting, using their voice and resources to ending this evil that has plague our society for far too long. I applaud those individuals who stand in the gap amid adversity promoting unity, goodwill, and love among all people while standing for justice. Thank you for your dedication to make our world a better place for all of humanity.

Acknowledgement

I sincerely thank my family and friends who stood by during this whole project. Your support and encouragement made this possible and I thank you all from the bottom of my heart. God Bless You and God keep you all.

Preface

The death of George Floyd has shaken the world and finally forced us to demand justice for black people. As a pandemic has hit the world, we now have the time to reflect on our conduct towards minorities. Spending time with our families in this uncertainty has developed sympathy in our hearts. We felt that sympathy when the video of a white police officer kneeling on the neck of George Floyd was release. Mr. Floyd could be heard saying again, and again, "I can't breathe," but the police officer did not stop, and one more innocent black person was choked to death. This incident is not the first of its kind. Too many black people have succumbed to this unfair treatment and have ended up either dead or arrested for either nothing or petty crimes.

This book is a source of awareness and a voice, not only for black people but also for every person who feels left out or discriminated against, on the pretext of his or her color, race, gender, nationality, or socioeconomic status. The topic of racism is universal. People from all over the world of any religion, status, race, color, and nationality face inequality and bias in some way. Through this book, they can relate their experiences and grievances. The protests across the world on the death of one black person is the clear message for everyone that humanity is on a united front to fight racism and racist people.

The motive behind writing this book is for those great and selfless people who have dared to speak up for their rights, the people who have sacrificed their lives to get justice for people of their community. This book is for those who, despite oppressed circumstances, came out to be bright personalities because mishaps reaffirm their mission in life. This book pays tribute to all the innocents who became a victim of racism and discrimination. I hope that this book inspires youngsters to bring light and change for those voices silenced by social hatred and prejudice.

In this book, we will describe how systematic racism affects a black person's daily life. How stereotypes make them feel like dangerous citizens or criminals, and how a racist society depraves each person of color of their right to life, freedom of speech, economic wealth, and accessibility to education and politics. Additionally, the book contains possible solutions to racist practices.

There are three distinct but related aspects of racism. Those are prejudice, discrimination, and stereotypes. Prejudice feelings stem from the emotions of anger and hatred toward the other group because of preconceived ideas about them fed by history and society. Discrimination is the behaviour of an individual where they think that outsiders do not deserve the same rights as themselves and exploit them through every means possible. Stereotyping means judging another person based on their beliefs without knowing or studying the truth and facts. Racism is a socially constructed concept based on race. It covers a wide interconnected web of political, social, cultural, and economic structures that secure the power of the dominant and majority race through the unequal distribution of wealth, resources, and opportunities. Racism is a serious global issue haunting the world right now, harming both individuals and communities without any reasons or excuses. The sociologists and anthropologists are still trying to answer the question: why is racism wrong?

Racism sparks injustice and hostility. It violates the principle of equality and justice, justifying the oppression of the weak. On an individual level, it destroys the mental health of black people. They feel left out, alone, sad, depressed, and fearful. They develop trust issues, affecting their social lives, and they become apprehensive and doubtful about people, even those who are sincere to them. They show this mistrust by staying away from public gathering, staying home from school, a workplace, or even shopping for fear of being verbally or physically attacked. This fear and doubt is a severe setback to their future goals and plans. When a person is afraid to socialize, participate in public, or feel demotivated to succeed in a given field, it is because they know that a white person will snatch every opportunity of success. Because of racism, promotions cannot be merit-based but instead based on color, race, and nationality. When denied jobs, admissions, and political participation due to racism, black people question their capabilities. A black person has to struggle with discrimination at every step. They have limited access to healthy food, substandard health care, and understaffed hospitals, poverty, and unhygienic living conditions make them vulnerable to deadly diseases. Compared to white people, the death rate of black new born babies is higher. Compelled to work under harsh conditions for long hours, and in cases of accidents in the workplace, black families do now receive compensation.

At the community level, racism does not affect one or two. It affects the whole community, neighbours, friends, and colleagues. America is a diverse country where people of different races, colors, and cultures are living but the hostile attitude of white people towards people of color creates hurdles for harmony and peace. Racism gives birth to a society where people hate each other. There are trust issues between races, and as a result, violence. The people are not able to raise their voices against brutality and discrimination. Innocent people are choked to death by the police, which is supposed to protect and serve citizens, whether white or black. Racism is poisoning our society. We sow the seeds for an environment our upcoming generation will live in, where they will breathe hatred and contempt. Racism has both adverse physical and psychological health consequences. Individuals make up a society, so how can we expect society to be healthy and prosperous if its members are physically and psychologically ill?

The underlying belief of racism is that black people are inferior and imperfect human beings because of their skin color, their history, culture, and language. Racism can be intentional or unintentional. People deliberately degrade black people because of their superiority complexes. They use their white card to show that white people are the only valuable asset and sincere citizens of America. While black children are bullied in schools, because of their background by the children of racist parents, who inculcate these stereotypes and beliefs in their child's mind. Sometimes, racism is unintentional; people have no idea that their behaviour is hurting the sentiments of black people. People unconsciously prefer a white lifestyle, so they apply creams to lighten their skin-tone or reject a person with dark skin. An example of unintentional racism is when a white woman clutches her purse when a black man or woman sits beside her. This behaviour and thought process has to change. We should be able to look at another person without being suspicious because of this person's race. We should not consider someone a criminal because of the color of his or her skin. If we are ever going to address racism, this attitude and mentality have to change. It has to change now.

Introduction

Lately, it seems that as soon as I switch on the TV, and there it is. News that a white police officer has killed another black person based on suspicion, usually after torturing them. That or a white man or woman, out of fear or hatred, has opened fire on a black person. Such incidents occur so often that even children understand and suffer because of this deadly disease of racial hatred of black people.

The Black Lives Matter movement regained its spark and thrill with the death of George Floyd. Since then, the world has started demanding equal rights for black people, and justice for anyone who has been wronged at the hands of the oppressors and racists. The last words of Eric Garner, George Floyd, and many other African Americans were the same: "I Can't Breathe." These are words uttered by a person experiencing difficulty breathing. They were unable to breathe both figuratively and literally. They have been choked off from their freedom, right to an education, to success, to celebrate, to feel free, and to be alive. The ever-increasing social prejudice and hatred are not allowing them to take a breath in an atmosphere where they are treated like human beings with equal rights.

Black people have been labeled criminals, drug abusers, thieves, robbers, and kidnappers for centuries. They have to bear the humiliation and insult because these labels are illogically attached to their skin color. An innocent black person on the street, at a shopping center, or grocery store is a threat in the eyes of the police. At schools or colleges, black students are given harsh punishments compared to white students for the same mistakes and behavior. It has become an instinct for white women to clutch their purses if a black man passes by or sits near them. These stereotypes and mindsets need to end forever.

The criminal justice system of any country is establish to provide justice to all people without any regard to color or race. However, law enforcement agencies, judges, and police officers appear to conspire against black people. Black people are more likely to get arrested and beaten compared to white people. Judges give harsher sentences to black people and other people of color, causing jails to be full of innocent people enduring the hardship of punishment because they are unable to speak in their defense. At the same time, white supremacists who kill and harm black people are free to cause more troubles for the black community. This injustice puts a question mark on the integrity of the entire judicial system.

All black people want is to live peacefully with dignity and respect, without fear of being falsely accused and arrested, police brutality, or being murdered. They want to protect their loved ones from the hatred of an unfair society. They feel pain when their children are forbidden to interact with others based on their race. They are filled with anxiety, depression, and fear because they lack healthy food, decent health care, and good jobs. According to an estimate, black people have 22% fewer chances to get proper medical treatment and medication. Poverty, violence, humiliation can damage the personalities of any person, but black people have been facing such calamities daily without any sign of change or hope.

It is apparent that Black people are alone in their fight, and only they can save themselves and their future. Demonstrations and protests can continue for days or even months, but later nobody seems to remember the incident and goes on with the same racist practices. Politicians promise to bring change for black people, but the promises never become reality because they are made to increase their re-election chances. We need to take solid steps so that the blood of innocent people is not wasted, and no more blood is shed. A supernatural being is not going to come to fight against this racism, so we have to start at a small level to bring about positive change and to bring an end to racism.

Black lives have suffered torture, lynching, and cruelty by their white slave masters. Since then, the matter has done nothing but worsened and taken a more dangerous form of systematic racism. At every level, black people feel oppression, whether, in school, business, film, or public places, the inhumane and unequal treatment is visible, and nobody questions it. Police arrest and kill black people before any evidence proving that person is guilty, and when the truth is revealed, it is too late. This lynching by the justice system is enough to prove that America still is not a safe country for people of color. Innocent black people are resting beneath the soil while the guilty are roaming around with little to no remorse.

The current protests, violence, and toppling of statues is not a perfect solution. The world would be a peaceful planet if all human beings could come forward and join hands to fight racism and forget the differences in their colors, origins, cultures, etc. The situation demands unity and love. Hatred and contempt will only aggravate the situation further. People of all color deserve respect and position in society based on talent, intelligence, and hard work. No one should have the right to snatch the opportunities and rights from a person and exploit them for their benefit. Black children, youngsters, adults, and elders are waiting for the world to wake up from this deep slumber of superiority complexes and take a stand for equal rights as proclaimed in The Constitution of the United States and the UNs Universal Declaration of Human Rights. Colonialism and slavery are condemned, by people from all around the world, but when the issue of racism and the Black Lives Matter movement is brought to light, the same people are willing to justify it. Such people are of the view that black people are criminals, useless, and idle sections of society and deserve to be treated like this. Nevertheless, little do they know that being a useful and respectable citizen of a country has nothing to do with color, and this systematic racism is more illegal and brutal than colonization and slavery.

The book is written with extensive research touching all the aspects of black life. The possible solutions and future of racism have been discussed with different angles and points of view. This book is a must-read for those who are experiencing or observing racism and want to bring it to a permanent halt. This book describes real experiences elaborated and clearly expressed.

Table of Contents

Dedication iii

Acknowledgement iv

Preface v

Introduction xv

Chapter 1: Why All the Hate? 1

Chapter 2: Racial Differences 12

Chapter 3: Blood Stained Evidence 19

Chapter 4: I Can't Breathe 26

Chapter 5: 8:46 34

Chapter 6: "Mama" 43

Chapter 7: "I Just Wanna Live" 53

Chapter 8: The Pain of Being a Black
　　　　　　Man in America 63

Chapter 9: Black Men and the Criminal
　　　　　　Justice System 74

Chapter 10: The Brutality of Lynching 85

Chapter 11: Not My Heritage 96

Chapter 12: Label Me Not 103

Chapter 13: Why won't the White Church
　　　　　　　Engage the Race Issue? 113

Chapter 14: COVID-19: Danger for the
　　　　　　　African American Community 121

TABLE OF CONTENTS

Chapter 15: The Purpose Behind Taking A Knee...132

Chapter 16: Say Their Names 142

Chapter 17: "No One Is Going To Save Us,
　　　　　　But Us" 161

Chapter 18: Will Reparations Be Enough?................. 175

Chapter 19: We the People: Broken Promises 187

Chapter 20: A Time for Change 199

Bibliography..213

About The Author 217

CHAPTER 1

Why All the Hate?

As I switch on the news networks or open any social media source, I see and hear hateful rhetoric that seems to pour through our airwaves. Everyone seems to be angry and frustrated. They display their hate towards everyone who differs in any aspect, whether it be color, background, religion, opinion, etc.

Why all of the hate? For centuries, scientists and anthropologists have tried to learn the answer to this fundamental question: what trait do all people hold?

What characteristic is, in other words, universal to the human experience? Is it our love of music and dance? Is it our desire to be challenged? Is it our capacity for love? Is it the fact that every human being goes through the same emotions, such as anger, sadness, happiness, fear, or disgust? All that said, while those emotions are universal, they are necessary for our survival. There is another part of the human experience, which is common to us all, which is much more depressing. I am referring to hatred and, more specifically, racism.

Racism, in all of its various forms, is no doubt a quintessential part of everyday life. In our society, it is natural that some people engage in xenophobia when they meet people of other ethnic origins. However, just because racism has been so universal does not mean that it is necessary for happiness. We would probably be much happier if we did not have so much hatred boiling away inside of us. Letting out our anger indeed relieves stress, and fear can keep us safe in times of potential danger—but what good does racism bring us? When someone is racist toward a group, they do not listen to reason. They are more likely to provoke arguments, become angry, and put others down. When hating other people or communities, they are trying to prove themselves superior and better than that person or community. These feelings are likely to spark riots and violence because other people will fight back. Nowadays, increased violence and bloodshed are the results of racism and superiority complexes.

Although we speak of slavery as part of the past, nowadays, it has taken a crueler role, which is systematic racism. In systematic racism, certain groups are systematically denied privileges based on their skin color. Although it is illegal to deny someone his or her due rights, based on their skin color, this law is just on paper. In reality, whether it is in the educational system, economics, or political field, people of color are ignored as if they do not exist. People of color—just like the LGBT community, and people belonging to non-dominant religions—are more likely to be attacked, assaulted, and robbed by those who promote hatred. Moreover, they receive less aid and funding, even though their communities might need it the most. They are stereotyped as being less intelligent or not as educated as their counterparts.

Suspected of crimes that they have not committed, minorities are detained, questioned, and arrested for long periods without proper legal representation. Compelled to live in underdeveloped areas, they live where poverty and overcrowding exists. In these areas, not only are the citizens much more likely to fall prey to substance abuse problems due to their impoverished upbringing, but the lack of funding offered also makes them more likely to develop mental illnesses. For example, statistically speaking, Native American youth who grow up on reservations have a significantly higher risk of committing suicide.

So, why do people engage in racist behavior? Well, in many cases, the perpetrators have been raised to distrust and dislike others who are different from themselves. This distrust is a large part of their identity. They have seen discrimination practiced by people they trust and love, such as their family, close neighbors, or best friends. Moreover, because they have grown up with these behaviors, it is easy to continue adhering to them after becoming an adult. Sure, they could change the way they act, but doing so is challenging. If people live in a context where everyone holds these same negative views, they might not see much of a point in changing a crucial part of their identity.

Another reason people treat each other with so much prejudice is that they enjoy validating stereotypes. Many people find it fun to make an assumption about someone and see it proven "true". I am sure we have all met people who criticize others because of their ethnic origins, pointing out that Asians are bad drivers, black people love watermelon, and white people cannot dance. When people start criticizing others in such a way, they are trying to reinforce their own identities by telling themselves that the stereotypes are true. Stereotyping props up their own identities and, by extension, their sense of self-worth.

Another reason we treat each other with prejudice is that our society stresses us out. Many things can frustrate us in a day—a global pandemic, the never-ending stream of work, our favorite sports team losing, missing an important appointment, the need to grab a bus at a specific time. When we get annoyed, we are more likely to become angry, and over time, this anger crystallizes into a form of hatred. For example, you might come to resent people who do not speak the same language as you. Therefore, you have trouble communicating with them at work, or you might resent people from another country because they keep beating your country at a national sport during the Olympics.

We also hate other races because we are fearful. When humans are in unfamiliar situations, their biological stress system gives them two options: fight or flight. Thus, when people live in societies where they do not interact with those of other races, they might be scared when they do and leave. As an example, consider that many white people feel threatened if they are sharing the sidewalk or elevator with a black man, especially at night. The other option, according to this evolutionary mechanism, is to fight. This reaction makes us more prone to arguing in public. Although both of these choices are biological, they are not helpful. Instead, we should resort to using our rational intelligence and tell ourselves that all humans are equal, and no person is inherently bad.

American culture has long encouraged racist practices. We need only to look at slavery, lynching, Jim Crow Laws, and the systematic erasure of the native people for proof. For a long time, even after they gained rights equal to those of white Americans, people of color were seen as inferior, less intelligent, or belonging to a different world. Politicians use the race card to gain the white vote by promising policies that aim at silencing the black community and their progress. Trump's decision to suspend immigration visas is an example of these instances. Time and again, he makes statements and policy decisions that direct at benefiting white people at the expense of ethnic communities.

According to the Pew Research Center, many Americans think that being white in the United States is a blessing because black people are treated less fairly in the judicial courts and are more likely to be killed in police encounters. In 2019, out of 1000 fatal shootings by police, 23% account for black people. Moreover, black people are likely to be arrested in drug abuse or drug dealing cases as compared to white people. According to a report, most black people have no hope that one day they will be able to enjoy the same rights and importance as white people.

Hatred and racism are omnipresent. It might seem like there is not a lot we can do about hatred given how ubiquitous it is. However, this is far from the truth. We can reduce hate every single day, even in small ways such as by treating others with kindness, respect, and watching out for those who are less fortunate. On a larger scale, we can contribute toward reducing hatred by joining an organization or participating in rallies. Either way, one fact remains true: we must stand together. We must build bridges between our hearts so that we can make the world a better place to live in for each of us. That is our task as human's beings here on planet Earth.

CHAPTER 2
Racial Differences

The United States claims to have gone into the post-racial era, but in reality, racism is a challenge that still affects the minority communities. Many races exist around the world, including blacks, whites, Asians, etc. Some individuals are favored while others receive discrimination. The late Dr. Martin Luther King, Jr. stated, "I refuse to accept the view that mankind is so tragically bound to the starless midnight of racism and war that the bright daybreak of peace and brotherhood can never become a reality... I believe that unarmed truth and unconditional love will have the final word." Many people view racism as a tool to cause destruction and division among society. The absence of inclusion and political factors are the primary cause of racism, which result in adverse economic and social consequences that may influence the ability of a nation to progress.

Over time, racial differences have led to marginalization and oppression of specific groups. Government administrations influence to address issues such as whether racial oppression diminishes or escalates. Through the development of policies and reforms, governments lay down fundamentals to counter racist acts by promoting fairness and equality. This work provides a clear analysis of the vital role power plays in countering racism in the community, relying on historical evidence to give more insight into the issue.

Despite governments being in a position to stop racial discrimination, harsh policies have been passed by these same governmental legislators to facilitate its existence. For example, Jim Crow Laws were used to oppress policies intended to address oppressive legislative in the late 19th and early 20th centuries, oppressed by the very system that was meant to defend and protect them. Blacks were denied the right to vote, mix in public places, and even intermarry with the white population.

Power plays a fundamental role in society as it can make things happen. For example, despite slavery abolishment in the United States, there has been continuous oppressive antics in the majority of communities as more African Americans face racial discrimination involving segregation and even police brutality. Violence triggers people to use the power at their disposal to counter injustices. This power resulted in the creation of the civil rights movements to air their concerns on the existing oppression. Activists such as Martin Luther King Jr. pushed for reform, leading to the formation of organizations such as the Equal Justice Initiative that work towards ending racial inequality, excessive punishments, and mass incarceration.

Black people/African Americans are certainly the most discriminated-against race in the world. The rate of bullying is high, and this is because they are the least socioeconomically powerful race. As is demonstrated in Jared Diamond's Pulitzer Prize-winning book, "Guns, Germs, and Steel," this lack of power is due to the isolation caused by the Sahara

Desert. This isolation prevents their race from having more than occasional interactions with Asians and Europeans and their technological and educational advancements over the centuries.

Many people of color have a deep distrust of white Americans because of slavery. In most cases, black people, for instance, feel that they have never been included in the development of the United States because a majority of those elected to better positions is white. A person of color has to work harder for promotions than white people. They must set their standards high, go to work, and be the best employee. Even if they are never promoted, they give their children, family, and friends a positive role model. Black women, for a long time, have felt like they have been neglected and not given equal rights as others have been, primarily regarding employment opportunities. Some argue, however, that there are black women who have been successful in different organizations and, therefore, if every individual worked hard, they could achieve the highest position. Black women, who have accomplished, motivated, and nurtured talent in the United States includes Oprah Winfrey, who is a media personality and entrepreneur. She has used her abilities and talents to open dialogue and discussion in the United States to help and nurture young talent and children in schools to work harder to be successful in life. The absence of inclusion increases inequality among minorities.

The world is in a constant struggle between the forces that want to maintain the status quo and the forces that seek to explore. People lose equal opportunities, which further widens the rate of inequality, affecting a majority of people across the globe. There is the need to control the acts of racism and thus promote a culture that does not discriminate. Race should not divide the human population. This division affects society negatively as individuals may seclude themselves based on color, creating disunity in the community and derailing the steps towards progress. Government officials should focus on implementing policies that drive towards equality.

CHAPTER 3
Blood Stained Evidence

Racism is a factor that has destroyed the lives of minority groups in the United States. The truth is, while movements like Black Lives Matter advocate for equal rights, there is a lot more to be done to end racism and hatred. Police officers have a history of violation within their power, such as making false arrests, maiming and killing civilians unnecessarily, and conducting crackdowns and search without warrants. The use of excessive force has been used extensively towards minority groups, raising suspicion of racism. Studies also show that racism extends to the health care area, a factor that has increased premature deaths of African Americans newborns.

The criminal justice system is biased and, as a result, leads to mass incarceration. According to Phys.org, the police kill every year approximately 1000 civilians. Out of these statistics, African American deaths account for three quarters. Unfortunately, only 1% of those officers face charges. Examples of these deaths include George Floyd, who died in Minneapolis. Evidence showed a white police officer kneeling on the neck of this unarmed individual, who was already under arrest. Floyd's death sparked days of massive protests across cities in the

United States. It raised the issue of race relations and police reforms. His death is not the only case that has raised the issue of racism. Eric Garner was killed in 2014 when a New York police officer subdued him to a point he could not breathe. Other deaths include Javier Ambler, who died after a vehicle chase in 2019 in Austin, Texas, and Manuel Ellis, whose death happened in March 2019 in Tacoma, Washington. Both of these cases are still under investigation; the families await prosecutions.

Minority groups are the most affected by police brutality. Police use excessive practices, such as the beating of suspects, destroying physical evidence, and shooting suspected criminals unlawfully. These actions paint a negative image on the police making them impossible to trust. The excessive use of force by the police is punishable by law, and the police face convictions for their deeds when found guilty. We expect the police to conduct themselves to ensure justice is served equally to all citizens by the law.

Statistics show the disparity in the serving of justice. Racial bias by police has led to increased protests witnessed across this country and the formation of movements such as Black Lives Matter. This increase took place with an increased rate in the deaths of unarmed black citizens by the police. From studies conducted in various states in the United States, there is a likelihood of 1 in 1000 black men will die from the use of excessive force by the police according to the La Times. These statistics depict the vulnerability of black people facing police brutality.

Additionally, most crimes done in this country, ethnic groups are the most unlikely to possess weapons compared to their white counterparts. The African American and Latino populations are more likely to be found in offenses of drug peddling and public misconduct. These are minor offenses compared to mass shootings, of which the offenders are mostly white. Most of the prison populations are African Americans and Latinos, which could either, be a result of police bias in making arrests or an unfair justice system. One argument against this is that this could be a result of most crimes are perpetrated by black citizens. If this is true, then a reason for this is due to unemployment, no economic or educational opportunities, and social status.

Walking on the street is no longer a right for African Americans, as one does not know if they will be arrested or shot by the police or some angry fearful white citizen. African Americans have been victims of torture. Countless videos show their arrest before being push to the walls or ground, causing injury. According to reports, many times, when police search for criminals or contrabands, they apply extreme measures that lead to the destruction of property. Most of these incidences happen to African American and Latino citizens. Reports indicate that police use discretion to search cars, and most of their suspects are African American.

Racism should not control the lives of the people. African American lives matter, and there is a need for reform to ensure that there are equal opportunities across the United States. Additionally, police in hot spot areas should create relations with the residents of these areas rather than intimidating them. These good relations would promote ease in solving crime and obtaining any necessary information. Changes will require educating the public and support of the minority groups. Equal opportunities and fair treatment will end fear and hatred, which have affected the lives of African Americans for decades.

CHAPTER 4

I Can't Breathe

George Floyd was brutally choked to death by a white police officer of Minneapolis. Hector Arreola, a 30-year-old man was killed in Columbia, Georgia, when a police officer sat on his back while another officer tied his hands to his neck and kept his face down for six minutes until he choked to death. In Phoenix, Muhammad Abdul Muhaymin died of cardiac arrest when four police officers sat on his head, neck, and back. Elijah McClain was returning home with groceries when three police officers strangled him until he vomited. In Staten Island, Eric Garner died when he was placed in a chokehold while being arrested by a New York City police officer. These are only a few cases; a list of police brutality on the defenseless and unarmed is long and tiresome. In all these instances, the last words of victims were, "I can't breathe." This simple phrase has become the international rallying cry against racism.

In the United States, police officers who are responsible for strangling, gagging, and choking people to death because of their color are left free. In most cases, no charges are rarely pressed against them. The repercussions faced by responsible officers are minimum. They even receive a short leave to escape the legal process. Charges are often dropped immediately instead of them being fired or arrested. The four police officers involved in the brutal murder of George Floyd have been charged but not adjudicated.

The United States Constitution states that every human being has a right to life, liberty, and opportunities without any regard to color nevertheless black people still have to protest for their basic rights. Black people have always been the victim of racism and discrimination; however, the death of George Floyd has moved both white and black people to protest across the world, whether it is in America, Britain, Spain, Nigeria, or any other country. People from all over the world are mourning and showing condolences for the tragic death and exhibiting rage against white supremacists.

The death of an innocent and defenseless black man is nothing new in history. There have been several incidents, but why has the death of George Floyd caused so much awareness? The reason is social media. Social media has been playing an important role in awakening the consciousness of masses that all lives matter through messages of sympathy and kindness, seen everywhere. They are affecting the stereotypes and thoughts of people. Now, nobody can get away with body shaming, color shaming, or criticizing anyone. We have seen the important personalities, including politicians, actors, artists, and sportsmen posted pictures to show solidarity with black people.

The hashtag #BlackLivesMatter is trending everywhere, but have we ever thought that these sympathies and words of kindness are only real in our statuses and posts. In real life, we practice racism. We prefer people of our color. We hesitate to mingle with people of other races and treat them as outsiders. The abolishment of racism cannot be abolished until we remove it completely from our minds and start seeing others as equals.

In society, the transfer of knowledge and information passes down from one generation to the next. When white people first colonized black people, stereotypes took shape and have passed down through generations. As a result, hardly a day goes by when we do not hear news about racist comments spoken by politicians including President Trump, media personalities, celebrities, business leaders, and those islamophobia attacks on Muslims and the killing or bullying of a black person by angry white citizens or the police.

When George Floyd uttered "I can't breathe" a few seconds before dying, he might as well have been using allegory to say that he was not only deprived of oxygen, but also from his basic right to life, protection, and freedom. He was choked to death not just by the deficiency of oxygen, but also from continuous oppression, stigmas, and maltreatment within society.

In educational institutions, black children are treated differently from white children, and the little souls have no idea why they are bullied and forced to sit separately. Black people are denied access to public gatherings. Their political participation is not encouraged. Black women are exploited more severely. They are used as sex workers, usually after being smuggled from their homes. They are kept as full-time maids to serve their white bosses and are deprived of educational and recreational facilities.

Not only black people, but also the entire human race are the victim of racism. Every person is exploiting another person at some level. The cries of "I can't breathe" can be heard from everywhere. Humanity is being choked to death and crying for help. We, as human beings, should feel the pain a person feels when he or she is not respected, and their life is considered unworthy. Yes, black lives matter just like white lives. If a black police officer had killed some white person, the reaction of higher authorities would not have been the same as this case. If George Floyd were white, he would have received a summon to appear in court. He would be walking around, alive, and interacting with his family and friends not buried six feet under ground while his family, friends, and the world mourn for him.

CHAPTER 5

8:46

Eight minutes and forty-six seconds is the exact time it took George Floyd to die while the police officer choked him with a knee on his neck. During the last eight minutes and forty-six seconds of Floyd's life, many activities were taking place in his brain, including psychological damage. As his system degraded, it led to an inevitable failure of chemicals released when random activity takes place, such as kicking legs as the body struggles to survive from shortness of breath. There is a possibility that Floyd's brain activity was ceasing the moment he called out for his mother. Nevertheless, unlike the heart, people cannot restart the brain.

When the brain dies, a person will not remember the events that have transpired. They are only trying to survive, which may be impossible, as was witnessed in the case of Floyd. When Floyd's brain stopped, no information was processing; there was nothing taking place in his brain; his brain became no more than a lump of a degrading tissue. If he had survived, the only thing he would remember was what happened before the brain stopped. After that, he would not be able to remember anything. Under this simulation, the brain cannot store or process information.

After the first four minutes of oxygen deprivation, the brain will start to die. This deprivation is exactly what happened in the case of Floyd as he shouted, "I can't breathe." With the interruption in the flow of blood, revival could have taken place within 30 to 180 minutes before his death. Even though there could have been some form of brain injury, but his life could have survived.

According to occult theories, a life is recorded; from the time, they were born up to their death. The brain plays an important role during the last moments of a dying person. In just a flash, a person will re-live thoughts and emotions, even the fleeting ones. Death is as quick as a burst of energy. That energy spills out the entire contents of memory before the consciousness dies. All this happens involuntarily and unfailingly for everyone. At that moment, one is simply unaware that they are dying. In certain conditions, one may know they are about to die, but not at the very last moment. They will not understand what is happening and why the flashbacks are happening. They will have no time to think or analyze it. They are not asleep but are unresponsive, one can reposition them, and there is no response whatsoever. They lose muscular control in their jaw, and their mouth falls open, it will remain open until the funeral home does their job. In the last moments of life, a person remembers their family, and this is evident in the case of Floyd as he cried for his mother. He probably thought that by mentioning his mother, there was a possibility that the officer kneeling on his neck would have sympathy and release him so he could breathe again.

Floyd's mind was going through a lot, including memories and thoughts of his mother, wife, and children. He thought about what he could do to change the situation. Had he acted differently, would he have gone through such pain? Would he still be struggling to survive while three officers and a crowd watched him cry that he could not breathe? No one decided to jump in and save his life. What a sad way to end his life when he could have survived, had he stayed at home that day. Was coming outside the reason his life would end? Were his actions bad enough that no one would save him?

During the last moments of life, one may get emotional and connect with their inner God. Perhaps Floyd cried to God to forgive this officer, for he did not know what he was doing. We learn in life that it is God who gives life, and He should be the only One to take it. Floyd died in pain for eight minutes and forty-six seconds.

Someone holding their breathing would become distressed; any person who has not witnessed this occurrence may get scared at first, but someone aware of what is happening would know that the individual is in distress because they feel discomfort and worry. The officers standing on the side could have persuaded their fellow officer to get off the neck of Floyd so that he could breathe easily without obstruction, and it could have saved his life. It is wrong for a person to exert pressure on another to the extent that they shout that they cannot breathe and not attempt to remove the pressure on his neck.

Breathing becomes very shallow, and there are long periods where the person stops breathing before starting again. As the body realizes its dying, it pulls the blood away from the extremities to the core.

This pull of blood causes toes, fingers, knees, and elbows to become cold and develop a purple lacy look called mottling. Not everyone mottles, and sometimes it comes and then goes, but it is a strong indicator that death is around the corner.

One moment your loved one is breathing, and the next moment, they are not. Anyone can feel uncomfortable with death and, in the case of George Floyd, someone should have jumped in to attempt to try and see if they could have saved the life of Floyd.

When a person dies, they almost immediately develop a pale-yellow hue. No one knows what one goes through at this stage in life. You would have to go through it to have the answer. Still, there are different theories about what someone goes through in general terms. People sometimes have serious accidents in their lifetime and, it could be said that they come close to those last few moments of life. These are known as near-death experiences. In them, it can be said that one is so close to death that they may sense the end of life. It is said that these late stages of life can be quite calm with an intense peacefulness. If this is true, then when one does get to this stage, there is nothing to fear at all.

Most people fear death, and when these last few moments of life do arrive, it is quite a surprise to see that there is such calmness. Why all the fear? The idea of seeing things that have happened to you in the past is striking. Some memories are good and others bad. These visions are said to feel very real, but they are just that; visions.

No one deserves to die as George Floyd did, choking for eight minutes forty-six seconds. There was plenty of time for someone to jump in and help. We all deserve a second chance; if a person has been arrested and committed an offense, then the police officers should let them go to court rather than kill someone. There is a lesson that we have all learned from this incident: life is precious and every second counts and people who stand by can do something to help.

CHAPTER 6

"Mama"

American has a long history of police brutality against black Americans. The major reason behind this brutality is the anti-black sentiment that is very dominant in most of the police departments in the United States. The recent murder of George Floyd ignited anger and fury in black people all over the world. The video of his death went viral and made people demand justice for this murder. Though this act of brutality was not something new in the United States, people reacted to it so strongly because they knew that if they stayed silent today, a time would come when they or someone they know or care about would end up like Floyd.

The video captured by a bystander shows that Floyd was unarmed as the white police officers showed off their power and superiority by handcuffing his hands and lying him down on his stomach. As the scene unfolds, we openly see many bystanders inform the police officer to stop putting unbearable pressure on Floyd neck as his nose starts bleeding. Floyd even repeated that he could not breathe, but nothing budged the officer until Floyd died. As Floyd might have realized that he would not survive this cruelty, he called out for his mother.

He called, "Mama," twice while taking his last breaths. He also said, "My stomach hurts, my neck hurts, and everything hurts," before dying after a few torturous minutes. His last call to his mother showed the power of unconditional love between a mother and her child. Every time we are injured, feel lost, alone, or troubled, most of us call out for our mothers because we know that no matter where she is, she will come to ease our pain and suffering. No one in the world can give someone as much love as a mother gives to her child.

In every phase of our life, whenever we need guidance, we look for our mothers. Floyd's mother died two years ago, yet he called for her in his last moments. He thought that she would come to rescue him from this brutality. Floyd's call to his mother proved the connection with his departed mother. Seeing a 46-year-old man calling to his mother while pleading to let him live broke the heart of many black mothers. They felt his pain while imagining their child being in the same position as Floyd. These mothers say that when he said, "Mama," they felt as if their children were calling out to them for help.

As we grow older, we become busy with life, yet our mothers take care of us without expecting anything in return. We do not realize their value and love until we give birth to our children and feel what it is to be a mother. We then understand the importance of the struggle that a mother goes through to keep her children safe, happy, and to fulfill their dreams.

The mothers who were touched by Floyd's words left their houses to protest and became the voice of his mother to demand justice for his murder. Floyd's death fueled people, and many protestors joined the movement Black Lives Matter to demand a race-blind society where their skin color did not define who they were. This death opened wounds of many black mothers who had lost their children due to the brutality of the police. They felt the pain and loss all over again. They imagined their child going through the same feelings of terror while taking their last breaths.

During an interview, Kadiatou Diallo, a mother of a black son who was shot dead in New York City by New York police officers, said, "As the mother of Amadou Diallo, having to suffer my loss on February 4, 1999, my wound was opened again." Amadou Diallo, a 23-year-old innocent boy, was living in New York as an immigrant. New York City police officers fired at him 41 times outside his residence, on suspicion without any solid proof. He did not have any criminal history, yet the police shot him dead because his real crime was that he was born with black skin and was among those with white skin.

No one is born with his or her own choice. We do not choose our skin color, facial features, or even birthplace, yet people act as if they had created themselves, or they had created their skin color! Skin color does not make anyone superior over another person. No one should be judged based on their skin color, as this world is for all people as much as it is for white people.

Another black mother, Gwen Carr, lost her son, Eric Garner, six years ago when a police officer choked him as he too died saying, "I can't breathe." She felt like she had lost her son again when she heard the words, "mama," from Floyd's mouth. During her interview, she said, "It's hard enough we're coming up on the anniversary of my son's death, and now to hear about this young man. It's like déjà vu; it's like the murder of my son all over again. He was basically the same age as Eric." She further said that she wishes that George Floyd get the justice that her 43-year-old son, and a father of six children, could not receive.

We felt the pain of Emmett Till, Freddie Gray, Breonna Taylor, and all other innocent black people who were killed for having black skin and living in a racist society. Like Floyd, they must have called out to their mothers while taking their last breaths. They must have recalled the protection and love that only their mother could provide at any moment of terror and pain, but the cruelty of a white-dominant society did not allow them to cherish that love ever again. Those who were hired to protect and serve them killed them, yet these same officers failed to perform their duty.

Every mother cherishes the word mama more than anything, so when their children call, "mama," when in pain, she will do anything in her power to free her children from whatever is hurting them. No matter what your skin tone, if you were a mother, you would never want your child to go through the same experience that George Floyd went through. It is your duty as a mother and as a human being to raise your voice against racism. We must become the voice of all those who never got a chance to prove their innocence and died.

We cannot let another brutal act by the police get by without getting justice for all black people killed for no reason. The earth is a free place. No one can have superiority over any other human being, based on his or her skin color. We were born free and will die free; no one can take this right away from us. As humanity is becoming endangered, we all must preserve and save it from becoming extinct. We cannot let our future generations face the same horrors of a racist society. We cannot allow future mothers to see their children struggle to breathe and say, "I can't breathe," as they die.

If we consider this incident as if nothing happened or choose not to raise our voices, as we have before, we will become victims one day. We, or our children, could be the next George Floyd if we do not fight for equal rights now. Cruelty should never be accepted, no matter what. We will never let the lives of George Floyd, and others like him, go in vain as it will be a cruelty to the innocent. It is the racist system that must be killed and not the harmless black people. It is the mentality that we must remove from its roots and not the minorities living in the United States.

Buried beside his mother in Pearland, Texas, we hope that George Floyd is with his mama in a peaceful place where no one will ever judge them based on their skin color again.

CHAPTER 7

"I Just Wanna Live"

The day after the murder of George Floyd, a 12-year-old boy, Keedron Bryant, shared a heart-melting video in which he sang the song, "I Just Wanna Live." Viewed more than three million times, the video has caught the attention of people around the world, including Barack Obama, Will Smith, Janet Jackson, and Kirk Franklin. The message of the song is too strong to be ignored. The song is three minutes and eight seconds of disclosures of the fear and pressure under which black people have to live. Keedron Bryant is at the age in which children's life is all about play and fun. They should not have to worry about whether they will live or die just for being black. However, a black child cannot be carefree. They have to face continuous prejudice at schools, playgrounds, and public places. They desire to receive the same love and treatment as white children get, but racist people will not even spare children. The voice of Kedron is the voice of all black children demanding their basic right to live. Black people from an early age experience discrimination, which makes them depressed and nervous.

Racism has a more adverse impact on children than adults. It not only affects their health, owing to a failed healthcare system but also their chances of achieving their goals. Racism is a disease that makes opportunities more accessible when based on the look of people. Biologically and genetically, all human beings are the same, which implies we belong to one race. The color of skin or the country we originate from should not matter. Nevertheless, throughout history, human beings have found excuses to differentiate them from other humans and then mistreat and abuse them. Colonization and slavery are the results of racism, white people think of themselves as far better than Africans, Asians, and other colonized nations, using this superiority complex to persecute and terrorize them.

"I Just Wanna Live" is a song by a 12-year-old boy and his experiences of daily life. It is the story of thousands of black children who are abused and harshly treated without knowing where they faulted. The child knows that no one on earth is willing to help him, stop this brutality, and speak for his cause on world forums. He asks for divinely help that God will protect him from His creatures who have become thirsty for blood. This boy should be in a tension-free phase of life, worrying only about his toys, books, etc., but he is worried about his life. Whether he will be able to see the next morning, go to school, and play with his friends.

Black children are the victim of racism before they are even born because of the stress and anxiety common for black women and poor maternal healthcare, resulting in low birth weight or other abnormalities. Fear and bullying can cause chronic stress, leading to hormonal changes and body inflammation. Black children, more often, come into low-income households. Therefore, there are rare chances for them to get a quality education, healthy food, or a hygienic environment.

Black people are not any less than white people in terms of mental capabilities. They are smart, intelligent, hardworking, and sincere in every field. No matter what profession they belong to, whether they are teachers, politicians, business people, entrepreneurs, or doctors, young black people are trying to make their mark but are not appreciated. They encounter setbacks because of their origin. The up-and-coming generation wants to prove their worth, to stand at the point where they can shine, but when they look around at the violence and inequality, they are heartbroken. It is their right to secure a stable financial position, to gain social respect like white people. However, blindfolded by racism and a sense of superiority, this society cannot bear the fact that a black person can achieve a height of success, even if they deserve it.

Black people have no justice, even in the criminal justice system. The police take an oath, before joining the force, to protect and serve every individual and punish the criminal regardless of their race, color, or origin. However, there is a stark difference between expectation and reality. Some police officers and departments are racially prejudiced, an event to the extent that they frame and kill innocent black people. Framed for selling or using drugs in schools and universities, destroying their academic careers: black teenagers are more likely to turn to illegal activities to make a living. The black neighborhoods are raided frequently and searched brutally without considering privacy and legal search warrants. However, in emergencies black neighborhoods are ignored completely.

All Black people want is to be able to spend their lives without the threat of being kill at any given moment. They want to protect their children from the plague of racism. Children are exceptional observers. They can sense when something is wrong with their parents. Seeing their parents distressed affects their academic performance and emotional stability. Black parents do not want a life like this for their children, but in the end, their children will face the same destiny.

It is depressing that Black people have to live under the constant shadow of death, as it is looming over their heads. They do not know if they will go home to enjoy family dinner or end up in jail at the end of the day. Black people are six times more likely to be arrested than white people. If a black person is at a crime scene, they are arrested without explanation and are denied the right to hire a lawyer. They usually end up with years of imprisonment without any proof or evidence. A safe place does not exist where they can explore opportunities freely and with surety that their hard work and struggle will pay off. There is no guarantee they will not be brought down because of their skin color or race.

At school, black girls are badly bullied and humiliated by their white classmates, but authorities remain silent on these matters. The law enforcement officers in schools or universities keep biased behavior with black students. In some report cases, white teachers treat black children differently. They misjudge their abilities and intelligence and inflict harsh punishments for small mistakes. Moreover, teachers play a major role in boosting a child's confidence. Otherwise, a child loses belief in themselves, influencing their future. Unlike other students, they cannot roam in hallways in their free time or have their lunch at the cafeteria because of the fear of segregation and insult. They are deliberately given lower scores on exams to stall their academic growth and lower the confidence in themselves. No black person, especially a child, should lose hope in themselves that nothing will change for them. Instead, black parents should talk openly about racial differences and prepare their children to speak up for themselves if someone intends to humiliate them based on their skin color, not violently but with reason and logic.

No black mother should ever be afraid or panic before sending their child out the door for school or play. They should not have to worry if their child will return alive or dead. Then when their child is murdered, to make matters worse, justice is let alone. The victim and his family are accused of criminal activity to justify cold-blooded murder.

We need to find ways to guide and train black children to raise their voices, to stand against racism, and not be a silent observer of cruelty and brutality. Black parents should not have to hide their children at home for fear of a racist world because it will further strengthen their racist beliefs. A change in the system demands active participation and presence. The younger generation should be filled with the spirit to alter the course of thinking toward the truth that all human beings are the same, and this black-white contrast should be discarded.

CHAPTER 8
The Pain of Being a Black Man in America

To be a black man in America is like fighting every day to mask your fears, worries, discomfort, and tiredness to look stronger and braver in front of the world that is trying to crumble you slowly. A black man do not know when they will be chased, grabbed, and held down with a knee on his neck and back or a gun pointed at their head because having black skin is a crime. They will die without a chance to speak for themselves and prove their innocence to the world.

In America, a black man does not only have internal battles, but he fights with the external forces that have worked against him for centuries. Black men live in danger just for existing in an anti-black society. They remain in a constant state of fear and anxiety in a racist system that continues to remind them that their lives do not matter. Even though they were born and raised in America, they will never be accepted equally or treated fairly.

Even if the United States Constitution states that black men are American citizens, and promises them equal opportunities and rights, they will always be treated differently, in every phase of life. They feel worried, scared, and anxious not only for themselves but for their children, innocent and unaware of the sin of having black skin in a society ruled by lighter-skinned people. America may seem like a land of opportunities but ask a black man, how he sees it. He struggles to live a life full of freedom each day. He looks contemplatively at the white people laughing and walking freely in the streets without fear of being assaulted or killed. He wishes to be understood, valued, and treated equally.

Even when he tries to let go of all internal suspicions and come out without fear of being bullied or mistreated, an incident like that of George Floyd's happens and reminds him of all the insincere words spoken to him. He remembers the words that receive no follow-through. The promises that usually are broken. The assurances that have always failed to come true.

If you were born in America, raised in America, and served your whole life helping America become better, then the world will see you as a great American. However, is this the same way other Americans see you? No matter what you do for your country, its citizens will identify you for your skin color first. It does not matter how much you have served this country and its people; no power can shield you from the everyday racism in the United States.

A black child going to school who always gets good grades yet receives backhanded compliments from their teachers. Their hair, skin, or different attitude makes them different from other students. Are not we all humans born like that? Billions of people are born and raised differently around the world. Society should not use uniqueness to humiliate or make anyone feel inferior just because they have a distinct identity. If you are black, you will face racist comments wherever you go. No matter if, you are a student, worker, celebrity, politician, etc. A society that has racism in its roots will not stop to show you its honest feelings, no matter how wrong they are.

Looking at the life of the former president, Barack Obama, a black American, we would come to know that even though he had power here in America, many people did not stop ridiculing him for having black skin. When he was running, as well as after the election, people asked him about his nationality. He is an American by birth, but this did not stop people from questioning the authenticity of his birth certificate. The current president, Donald Trump, who has never supported black people, once claimed that Obama lied about his nationality. He later changed his statement, but that did not change his intention to make others question his certifications.

Many people would not give President Obama the respect that he deserved. During an interview, a former advisor of Obama told the media that once a Republican disrespected Obama by saying, "You know, we don't really think you should be here, but the American people thought otherwise so we're going to have to work with you." Even though many people opposed him and took a stance against him, Obama proved himself. He showed the world that no power could destroy you if you are confident in yourself. He proved that your skin does not define you; it is your character that makes you who you are. Many other black politicians face the same racism in their corner of democracy. They serve their country even though they do not receive the treatment that they should.

According to CNN Business, when looking at Fortune 500 companies, there are only four black CEOs. This fact shows that black people are not given an equal chance to progress and succeed. Despite their hard work and diligence, they do not have the opportunity to thrive.

In addition, according to other studies, more than half of the African American corporate workers have faced racism in their offices at least once in their lives. Workers from different corporations shared their personal experiences in an interview.

Some overheard their colleagues making racist remarks while some felt left out in every meeting. Even though they experienced racism in different forms, they never stopped putting effort into their survival. Instead, the racist comments helped them become tougher, better versions of themselves. They learned through racism how to make their name without letting the system put them down.

There are different types of sports played across America. Many of the national teams have black players who have won several championships and gold medals and have made their country proud. Although, every time a player tries to raise his voice against injustice in America, authorities silence them either by kicking them out of the game or by some other means. The history of sports is full of many examples of this, from

Muhammad Ali to Colin Kaepernick, many athletes have used their platforms to make the unheard voices of the oppressed known.

Raising their voices against inequality put their careers at risk, but nothing could stop them because they knew they were in the right. They knew that someone had to take action to put an end to the brutality that black people have faced for centuries. Therefore, instead of waiting for someone else to come forward, they took that responsibility on themselves.

Black people are tired of fearing for their lives. The time has come to put an end to the repetition of the same brutal incidents. The racist tree, whose seed sown centuries ago, must be cut down at its roots. A new tree must be planted in its place, a tree that blooms flowers of love, hope, peace, and unity, a tree whose fragrance of freedom spreads miles and miles.

However, there may be some people who may call you black, but it is their hearts that have gone black, and that is the real blackness. The malicious blackness engulfs a person into a sea of unending cruelness. They will one day become a victim of their self-made hatred and cruelty.

Black men have lived a tough life. They have been traveling a journey that has molded them into who they are today; a better version of themselves. The circumstances pains, which they have felt have failed to put them now. Instead, the pain has acted as burning fuel in their veins that does not let them tolerate the injustice anymore. This fuel does not allow them to sit idle by in their homes while their sisters and brothers are being killed on the streets across America.

No matter what color skin you have, black or white, or any other, if you will not try to stop the discriminations of today, you too will be affected by a racist system one day. All humans have the same roots. We came from the same blood, so why discriminate. What divided us? What made us part ways and start pointing fingers at people of color for every crime? Black people have as much right to live their lives the way they want as white people have. The world cannot silence them anymore. They must win the fight that started years ago. We need to help build a fair and united nation rather than a cruel and divided nation. We can create a world of peace and love, and we can all be queens and kings of our own destiny.

CHAPTER 9
Black Men and the Criminal Justice System

The criminal justice system is an institution, which is responsible for maintaining law and order of a country. As a citizen, we come across the justice system daily, such as the police responding to a burglary and arrest the culprits. They are then taken through the court system where they are given a trial; this is an example of the criminal justice system. The primary purpose of the criminal justice system is to provide justice to all by punishing the guilty and providing safety to the public so that they can live in a society fearlessly. However, what if the system is biased and punishes innocent people because of the color of their skin while letting go of the real criminals who are responsible for crimes.

The Policing of black men and women is a common theme in America. The criminal justice system in America works differently for African Americans. According to an estimate, in 2019, out of 1000 deadly police encounters, 23% involved a black victim. For African Americans, police have the policy to shoot first and ask questions later. The recent incident of the death of George Floyd and the shooting of Jacob Blake at the hands of two white police officers is nothing new. Before him, many innocent African Americans have lost their right to life because of their skin color. They are choking to death under the pressure of social hatred and contempt. Despite brutality and inequality in every field, police bias and torture has sparked outrage in African Americans because police are supposed to serve and protect all citizens, regardless of their race. The real fault lies in the system.

There was a time when black men were lynched just for being black, being in the wrong neighborhood, for speaking to a white person in an angrily tone, for bumping into a white person, or for not using a proper title or showing respect while addressing a white man. When a black person steps out of their home, they have to act in a certain way to ensure the police and public understand they are not a threat. Those who fail to do so suffer the consequences. Orders come from a higher authority to treat

African Americans in a way nobody would consider ever treating white people. This treatment includes beating, handcuffing, pepper spraying, choking, unlawful detaining, using dogs to subdue, and killing. Patrols take place in predominantly black neighborhoods without any reason or suspicion. Black People are dragged out of their houses, beaten, and jailed without proper cause. On the other hand, white communities are patrolled, regularly for safety purposes and the protection of those within the community.

Looking back on the past, in the 17th century, Africans were kidnapped, enslaved, and brought to America under harsh circumstances. After slavery ended, it took other ugly forms, one of which is racial injustice. There are more African Americans in jails and prisons than white people, who serve harsher sentences and, most of their time, are locked up for crimes they never committed.

In addition, there are constraints for black Americans called to jury duty because of socio-economic conditions and legal inequalities. White judges are preferred over black judges because they are allegedly more honest and trustworthy. The sin white judges commit while giving sentences, which effects the life of the black person and his family. There is a code of conduct for United States judges. According to this conduct, the judges are expected to perform their duties with respect and honor and should refrain from biased, prejudiced judgment.

Black women and girls have to suffer more discrimination because of their gender, but their experiences remain largely hidden. For example, in 2005, a five-year-old black girl, Jaisha Aikins, was arrested at her school for displaying anger, which is common in children her age. They handcuffed her because she hit the vice-principal of the school. He was not hurt since a child cannot hit very hard, yet they still dragged her to the police station in handcuffs. This incident shows how the police harass the black community, no matter how young and harmless the situation is. The interference of law enforcement officers in schools has caused much trouble for black students. Several cases have been reported by the New York Civil Liberties Unions, in which black girls were pushed against the wall, beaten, tortured, or abused for leaving the class early or roaming in the hallway. Black girls and women also experience the most sexual harassment and derogatory comments. In other words, black women come across every form of violence and misconduct at the hands of police, whether they are in schools or on the streets. There is no safe place for them.

In rare cases, police officers are convicted for the murder of innocent lives, but they are set free or given a temporary suspension more often. Racial inequality penetrates the criminal justice system. From cops to judges, the system is full of discrimination and racism. Robert Staples, a criminologist who authored the article, "White Racism, Black Crime, and American Justice," he argued that the criminal justice system is the invention of white people to serve the interest of white people, while humiliating and punishing people of color. Staples charged jurors and judges of giving biased punishments. African Americans are more likely to be arrested for drug abuse or street crimes based on suspicion, as compared to white people. There is also disproportionality in reduced sentences based on plea-bargaining between white and black people. Black people have to endure longer and harsher punishments compared to the same crimes also committed by white people. Judges use discretion when sentencing black people. If the victim of a supposed crime by a black person is white, the chance of more severe punishment is high.

This discrimination and inequality serve the interest of elitist white people. This mindset brings monetary gain in the form of fines, case expenses, or probation fees while also benefiting white people in multiple ways. Issuing arrest warrants against black people for insignificant street fights or even on the innocent decreases their chances of employment or having the right to vote because of a criminal record. In this way, the chances of employment for white people is higher. The racist politicians run the election campaigns by vowing to introduce policies and plans aimed at benefitting white people at the expense of exploiting black people to win the votes of a white racist.

While the victory of Barack Obama as the first black president of the United States of America was an exciting step in political equality, as soon as Obama took office, criticism met him for every decision made. He received accusations for being a socialist and repeatedly compared to Hitler. The public charged him with using racial anxiety for political gain. Many claimed that he is endorsing jihad culture because he supported Muslims. Despite his remarkable presidency and progressive policies, he still was regarded as a threat by white racists who simply could not digest the fact that a black American could sit in the White House and make important decisions for the country.

America is a supposed to be a diverse country where people of all different races can interact with one another. However, police and judiciary systems consider anyone non-white as a threat to the peace and security of this country. The last words of George Floyd, "I can't breathe," have been enough to awaken higher authorities from the slumber and sense of superiority. This phrase has become symbolic to describe the harsh and severe conditions under which black people live. African Americans cannot breathe because of their lack of educational opportunities, employment, their right to vote, and the ability to hold a political office are choked away from them. Black Americans live under constant fear and terror. Black people are usually, not released on parole because of mistrust, while more violent white criminals are released on parole. America boasts of having a transparent judicial system, but all this is a hollow sham.

Hillary Clinton once asked a crowd of white people a bitter but honest question: what would their feelings be if the police treated them the same way they treat black people? There would be a conflict and revolution if police started patrolling white neighborhoods with the same violence they patrol black communities. Unless there are reforms in the criminal justice system, the death of George Floyd will not be the end. There will be more victims who die in the same manner as many others have.

CHAPTER 10
The Brutality of Lynching

Every time I see the word lynching, I am reminded of the many lives of black people who were brutally murdered for crimes that they did not commit. The intention of murdering African Americans was to terrorize the community and create fear among the people. Many of these lynching were for crimes not committed but happened because black people violated the hierarchy among racial groups.

Although that was in the past, but they still killed black people. They still live in this world of hatred, while white people tell black people they need to forget. They are labelled criminals and animals. How much longer must they suffer and die under tyranny? African Americans live under the pressure of physical, psychological, and economic oppression. There are mixed feelings on this particular subject. For one, we should be saddened and horrified to know that this pain still exists. We would not want anyone to witness this, especially children. Then again, we should show the sin of our nation so that we never forget the ignorance and hypocrisy that drove this hatred. In one way or another, everyone will be affected by knowing an innocent person has died. It is upsetting that a community could support these murders by doing nothing to stop them or seek justice for African Americans.

We have had to look at the monuments and statues dedicated to Americans who helped keep these atrocities in place. In Charlottesville, they fought to keep the statues of confederate soldiers installed, while the lynching of innocent black people by white mobs were the life-style they fought to preserve. Everyone agrees that we should not try to erase history, but people are referring to the side that they approve. No one ever faced justice for these murders, just as cops today carry out lynching of today. Remember, they kept records of public lynching, but not all killings of innocent black people.

One of the most compelling stories of African Americans that received lynching is the story of

Jesse Washington. Washington was a black seventeen-year-old farmhand who was lynched in the county seat of Waco, Texas, on May 15, 1916, in what became a well-known example of racially motivated lynching while people watched. There was community acceptance of the lynching, and people would even dress in their Sunday best to witness the murders of African Americans. Jesse was only a child; he did not deserve to die at the age of 17 with a cheering crowd watching on.

People do not talk about lynching, but they have seen these pictures and videos. Unless we show pictures and tell the stories, people will forget about the past, and that is the reason racism continues to affect black people in American to date in 2020. When hearing stories of families smiling during the torture of African Americans, it is hard to believe even women, who understand the pain of childbirth, would support such actions. How we remember our history determines the approaches that could end the victimization of African Americans.

Breonna Taylor, a 26-year-old female, was unarmed when police officers, while sleeping in her house on March 13, 2020 shot her eight times. The officers were executing a search warrant in a drug case, but since the victim was unarmed, there was no reason the death of Taylor should have happened. The officers escaped prosecution with a reassignment, and the case is still pending the results of an investigation. Another victim of murder is Atatiana Jefferson, who was shot in 2019 in Miami, Florida, while at home. She was shot through the window as the police responded to a call from a neighbour who reported that Jefferson's front door was open. Deaths like these can be avoided, but instead, they show the racial hostility that continues to exist and is affecting the African Americans community today.

Most recently, Jacob Blake, a 29-year-old African American male, was shot and wounded by a police officer of the Kenosha Police Department in Wisconsin on August 23, 2020. Four of seven shots fired at his back during an arrest by police officer Rusten Sheskey, as officers were attempting to arrest Blake. Blake was shot as he opened the driver's door to his SUV and leaned in. Three of Blake's sons were in the backseat.

These injustices need exposure on a massive scale to white Americans. We need to acknowledge the truth in our history, or we are doomed to repeat it. Racism in all of its forms still exists, and lynching takes the form of other injustices and killings of black men and women. Has there not been enough pain? It is time to change and heal this nation. It is time to banish the confederacy symbols because they were no heroes.

Lynching was a horrific act, and the saddest part of it is the fact that children took part in this evil practice, some of which are now the parents and grandparents of people still alive today. They have passed down the hatred they grew up with to their children. These people are now our teachers, doctors, lawyers, judges, politicians, neighbours, business owners, etc. These passed down emotions are why racism is still rampant. By knowing, we mean acknowledging with an understanding of how things happen to black people in America were evil and the long-term effects on a community or nation. It is like the husband who cheats on his wife, and she knows it. For them to repair their marriage, they must take certain steps, but the husband that says, "Yes, I know what I did, but I don't wanna talk about...you need to get over it so we can move on." African Americans have been through tough times, and they cannot move on.

America does not like to acknowledge the sins of slavery but acknowledge the sins of every other country including Hitler's Germany, which is still being played repeatedly at a time when black people were being publicly lynched, murdered, or subdued. We should feel shameful as a nation for not speaking out, hearing, or acknowledging the history of blood spilled onto the soil of this nation. The sins of America are catching up quickly,

I pray for this country, this government, and this business does not come to rest until we manage certain matters! It is time we talk about our real history and push it into the light. Unless people appreciate the pain of African Americans, it would be impossible to move forward.

The family, the children, and friends of George Floyd, who saw the video of his death, will be traumatized for decades. No one would want to watch another person die. If we do not want to watch someone dies, then why are other human beings taking the lives of African Americans because of hatred. One would ask, why is no one protecting the rights of African Americans? Some black leaders could come up with reforms to change the criminal justice system, but the leaders are representing their interest and not fighting for laws that increase equality and fair treatment (Lartey & Morris, 2020). Now, the rate at which police shooting and killing of African Americans is no different from the lynching's that took place during the time of slavery and beyond.

Since President Trump claims he has made America great again, it begs to question: at what point in history was America great? America has only been great for the few individuals who are part of the white community that buys into political slogans that he represents. America has far more to be ashamed of than it has to be proud of but, that is more truth than most Americans are, especially white Americans, want to accept. It is our duty as humans, and as Americans, to not look away, but to learn the facts. We must learn our collective history and work toward truth, reconciliation, and healing. Refusing to follow the law is a factor, which has contributed to the current injustices of African Americans. Therefore, we continue to witness the murders of innocent African Americans. People must understand that history cannot be unlived, despite the wrenching pain. African Americans ought to face the injustices with the courage to demand change, which will push for reform. African Americans do not deserve to die; they deserve a better life. They deserve to live, be respected, and treated like human beings like everyone else. When people come together in unity and working for the common good of all humanity, this will make America great. This is not just a slogan, but people of all races and backgrounds working together for the common good of all of humanity.

CHAPTER 11

Not My Heritage

Confederate flags and statues are being toppled off their pedestals by protestors each day across this nation. We continue to hear in the news about the removal of statues with racist connotations. People are expressing their hatred of confederate artifacts, but what is the point of creating a fuss? Removing these statues will not eliminate the suffering and pain inflicted on black people. The question may arise, what are these Confederate flags and statues, anyway?

In 1860-1861, eleven southern states parted ways with the rest of the United States to preserve the institution of slavery, the eleven states used many flags to show solidarity against racial equality, but one flag, known as the battle flag, became most notorious. To some, this confederate flag symbolizes southern heritage, while others regard it as the symbol of slavery and white supremacy. Even though many southern non-extremists see the flag as their heritage and as a tribute to their ancestors, to most Americans, the flag brings back memories of racial injustice by those who wanted to continue suppressing the voices of black men and women. The confederate flag is a message for the fighters of racial equality that equal opportunities are not for black people; black people are only slaves, not made for dignified lives. The flag is a reminder that no matter what, there will always be white supremacy.

The civil rights movement raised its head in the 1950s and 1960s, and in response, the confederate flag was hoisted again by many southern politicians and sympathizers.

Now, in 2020, after the various murders of black people by police officers, protests have built up again against racial discrimination. The protestors are not only black or colored-people but also white people who can see the pain and suppression endured by the black community. For them, the confederate flag and statues are not heritage, but a remembrance of hatred towards black people. We should remove these artifacts to send a clear message worldwide that we are united, and we want the abolishment of racial segregation.

As a result, public statues are under attack worldwide. In June 2020, statues of Christopher Columbus was attacked, beheaded, toppled, and thrown into the river in Boston and Minneapolis. A protestor viewed that Christopher Columbus Waterfront Park as a dedication to white supremacy and indigenous genocide. American Museum of Natural History recently decided to remove the statue of 26th president, Theodore Roosevelt. The monument depicts Roosevelt sitting on a horse flanked by one African American and one Native American. This statue is a symbol of racial hierarchy, in which two people of color on each side exhibit the superiority of the white man.

Political figures of the British colonial era are associated with racism as well. In the past, campaigns have been made to take down the statues of Mahatma

Gandhi, as he is criticized for considering black people inferior to Indians and, as a believer of racial segregation, endorsed ill-treatment of black people. Winston Churchill, former Prime Minister of the United Kingdom, was accused of racist remarks and held responsible for the death of three million people in Bengal because of inadequate policies and a desire to preserve its status as a colony. In June 2020, protesters attacked his statue in London. Likewise, a statue of Edward Colston, a British slave trader, was vandalize in Bristol, England.

These statues have haunted the world for hundreds of years and reminded us of the torture and injustice inflicted on people because of their skin color. Looking at these statues brings back the harsh memories of when the ancestors of black people did not have the fundamental right to live. For them, these statues are not the legacy of great men but a reminder to the world that black or people of color will never be welcome with open arms, and there will always be the dominance of the white nation. Many consider the removal of these statues as a step towards political correctness. They think that people all over the world need to forget these names, especially Americans. While other white nationalists call it a distortion of history.

The confederate flag and these statues are symbols of hate to those who want to maintain oppression; discrimination is their pride and heritage. President Trump, in order to increase his voter base, campaigns to make America great, but in reality, what he really wants is to make America white again. His racist remarks have brought controversy time and time.

Although removing the confederate artifacts helps send the message of racial equality and hatred for injustice, what about those who promote these symbols? The brutal legacy lives in their hearts. That is why they say a person can die, but ideology lives on. These people fight for their exclusive heritage, a heritage that does not include black people or people of color and their achievements. Therefore, to make America truly great again, we need to celebrate heritages of all people, irrespective of race. America can be great and successful when each person is given due rights without fear of humiliation and discrimination. This is a heritage that one can be proud of, when all are included.

CHAPTER 12

Label Me Not

Right from childhood, it is instinctive to label everything we come across. We place things in categories based on similarities and exclude others because of their differences. Unfortunately, this habit of eliminating or debarring others grows with us. When we interact in society as an adult, we look at other people with a different color, race, religion, country, culture, or ethnicity, and start labeling them as outsiders and dangerous.

The world is facing so many grave issues right now, such as a global pandemic, global warming, an economic crisis, poverty, ethnic genocide, etc. but people insist on creating distance and discrimination instead of working together to solve these problems.

Variety and diversification are natural. If everything in the world were the same, there would be no enjoyment. However, we cannot even tolerate a difference of opinion, so the brutal killings of people of color are not beyond our understanding. Adolf Hitler is considered a synonym for brutality and oppression. His contempt for the Jewish community made him one of the greatest villains in human history. Nevertheless, people still follow his ideology when we oppress people of color when we do not speak up for their rights when we snatch opportunities from them because of our superiority complexes.

Black people have had to deal with humiliation and discrimination since the days that they were taken from their homeland countries to be traded into slavery many centuries ago. Black people have always been the victim brutality, and they have been enduring this oppression from generation to generation. Unlike white children, black children are labeled as trying to be white if they speak proper English and called ghetto if they speak other dialects other than English. They are bullied and shamed by both students and teachers.

This labeling is not only a result of racism but is also psychological. Many white people try to project these behavioral traits on black people, which they do not want to see in themselves. Black people are assume to have a criminal background, live in poverty, no morals, and are only able to obtain low paying jobs. For example, a black man went to meet his friend at work, in a high-rise building. When the security guard at the front desk saw the man, he made him use the worker's elevator because he assumed he was a messenger. People mock their culture and history even though it was their ancestors, who provided hard manual labor for cheap. In colonial times, black people were brought from the continent of Africa to take up manual labor work, because white people thought of themselves as too superior for these jobs. In the time of apartheid, there was a racial hierarchy, in which white people were at the top, Indians and Asians in the middle, and Africans were at the bottom. Everything is according to this ranking, including rights and privileges. Even after the abolition of slavery, black people had to face the denial of civil rights and segregation laws. They were given different labels in different countries like nigger in America, macaco in Brazil, kallu in India, and hakgwai in China.

According to the Racial Disparity Audit performed by the government of the United Kingdom, as compared to whites and Asian people, black people are more likely to be detained in police custody for long periods. In many countries, black people are often stopped and searched without suspicion and arrested without evidence. Even in black-majority countries, such as South Africa, white people have a large percentage of the wealth and possession of 72% of the private farmland.

There is another label associated with black people. The term is Negrophobia, meaning the fear of black people. Black people are viewed as criminals or as part of a gang when seen walking down a street. When parents come to know that their child's teacher is a black person, they feel their child is unsafe and advise them to stay from their teacher or even register a complaint. People feel frightened at the sight of a black person so much that they feel the urge to call the police for their protection. For example, a video of a white woman calling the police on a little girl who was selling water bottles to save money for her Disneyland trip once went viral on the internet.

Other examples include a video of a white woman, nicknamed BBQ Becky, who called the police when she saw a black family enjoying themselves at a barbecue in the park. In addition, memes called Karen's memes can be found across the internet. These memes describe thousands of white women who take pride in using white privilege by venting their anger and frustration on everyone, including black people. There are many instances where white people go to the extreme, to harass or publicly humiliate black people by calling the police. Black people are beaten and arrested for no reason other than a white person judged them based on their skin color. In schools, white children fear their black classmates because of the teachings of their parents. As a result, they feel hesitant about befriending or even talking to black children. In universities and colleges, black students are search based on the assumption of the possession of drugs or weapons. White people avoid them in stores, and if any black person enters their neighborhood looking to purchase a house, they call the police to warn the black person not to rent or buy in their vicinity.

However, despite all this, the people are ready to start embracing differences and want to stop the hatred. The rallies and protests across the world have started the murder of George Floyd are proof of the change in mindsets. The protesters not only included black people, but people of every race, religion, or color are condemning this injustice. These people belong to different backgrounds and political preferences, but one thing that is binding them together is the love for humanity, regardless of color. Why are white people taking part in the marches and demonstrations against the police? It is because they know what our state institutions are doing to the minorities is not justifiable and is only a result of racial hatred. These people are not marching and raising their voices for only George Floyd; they are standing up for every black person whom every opportunity and right has been snatched away, just like their breath. Every black person cannot, breathe because society still has a grasp on their lifeline preventing them from living.

Social media is justified to receive credit for this progress and sense of belonging. People can now see the violence and incidents with their own eyes, which creates empathy, and when millions of people start talking about one thing, it gives them the sense of empowerment that they can speak for the oppressed and together, bring change. The fear that the same thing can happen with their loved ones gives them the strength and power to leave their homes to March, protest, and fight injustice. Additionally, there are dozens of television shows, documentaries, and movies that spread awareness about equality as they depict what black people have to go through daily when they cannot use their basic rights.

Not only black people, but also all minorities in general are consider voiceless and powerless all over the world. They must convert to the majority religion, we steal their lands, they cannot celebrate their culture freely, their women and children are not safe, and they do not have access to basic health care. The world is facing multiple issues. We should not be adding to the miseries of people but should be offering hope that will unite people for the common good of humanity.

CHAPTER 13
Why won't the White Church Engage the Race Issue?

Religion is one of the oldest and most conventional practices in the world today. There are many different religious groups, including Christianity, Hinduism, Islam, Buddhism, among many others. All religious groups proclaim to foster belief systems for people to enhance their spiritual growth. The Bible describes the role of Christianity and guides them in their faith. Billions of people follow the ideals of Christianity; they attend churches, and missionaries have spread the teachings to places such as America, Africa, Asia, and Europe. However, despite this large number of Christians throughout the world, there are still injustices done to worshipers, especially those who are minorities in nations such as the United States.

Evangelical Christians in the United States have failed to tackle the issue of racism in the church and outside. Recently, these Christian's response to the killing of George Floyd was unexpected. According to these Christians, the sins were in the individuals, not society. They think that belief is about personal salvation. Evangelical theologians are the biggest threats to racism because they reject the concept of a social gospel, which holds that we pursue the kingdom of God to improve the lives of everyone on the planet.

Racism has infiltrated religious organizations, and unfortunately, the people who could have stood up for equality have not even made progress in religious organizations. To begin with, content developed for mainstream media perpetrates cultural beliefs and values to reflect current happenings in society and influencing future perspectives. Most of the media networks tend to emphasize that African Americans are thugs, thieves, criminals, drugs addicts, and this has spread to the places of worship. African Americans cannot attend any church they desire, which denies them the freedom of religious worship as outlined in the constitution. It is unfortunate that the church preaches the word of God and teaches people how to love one another. However, they do not put forth the effort into accommodating minority communities. White American Christians could also intercede the issue of racial injustice on behalf of the minority groups, but they have never engaged in such conversations.

The current headlines connect to ancient atrocities, and it is clear that there is a similarity on the issue of race and the church. In one of the most influential polls in which Pew Research Center conducted in America regarding issues, such as how being African American feels in the United States, most of the findings show that many have developed feelings of being alienated, even from the church. In most cases, churches in the United States have reported as not diversely attended. There is much that can be done by the places of worship to ensure that they achieve goals of equality.

The gospel gives people hope, but it is evident from the statistics that there is no diversity in the white churches. The late Dr. Martin Luther King Jr. said that "Sunday at 11 is "The most segregated hour in this nation". People of the same color go to the same churches, so the minority communities have their own churches. The Bible encourages Christians to love each other as Christ loved the church, while most other religious organizations have different motives. The drive, it seems, is not to unite people, but to increase divisiveness among communities. It is unfair that some of the believers in these churches have developed the belief that African Americans are not good people. Unfortunately, if Christians and other religions do not create an inclusive policy to accommodate people of all races, then it may be impossible to end the issue of racism.

Some white parents teach their children not interact with other races, a factor that spreads to schools and workplaces. It is unfair to deny young children the right to be diverse and learn from other people. Unfortunately, most of the existing forms of religion are not focus on developing a culture of trust, which would improve the welfare and values of people. There is a need for reform in the church, but also in educating young people to love each other. When children are taught from a tender age to treat each other as equals, then there is little doubt that it will increase equality and fair treatment among all people involved. Changing the mindset of young people is the only way to end racism.

White Churches ought to rise and advocate for the fair treatment of minority communities. The white church is silent about these issues while people continue to brutalize and dehumanize. The white church could use these situations as an opportunity to develop an approach to resolve the gaps while guiding people to God. It is discouraging to see people fail to treat each other equally, yet minority communities contribute so much to the development of the nation. Churches should be pillars to mentor individuals to succeed in the future and not be a place of creating divisions.

The concept of injustices of African Americans stems from various aspects of religious dimensions. For starters, there is a misunderstanding of the character of an African American. The concept of racism continues to perpetuate injustices to African Americans, as it increasingly penetrates other areas such as the political, social, cultural, economic, and educational sectors. We must create measures to minimize the threats and improve the lives of African Americans who have been affected by racism. These measures will create a culture of understanding while promoting equality and fair treatment of individuals across the globe.

CHAPTER 14

COVID-19: Danger for the African American Community

African Americans face inequality in many areas of life. One area is the provision of inadequate healthcare services. This inadequacy is not something new; they have been receiving limited services for centuries. A major cause behind this is racial discrimination that is deeply rooted in America. Due to this discrimination, not only patients but also black healthcare workers receive the worse treatment than the treatment that white patients and healthcare workers receive.

As the COVID-19 pandemic hit the world, many countries faced an economic crisis. There are three working groups: those who lost their jobs completely, those essential workers who could continue their low paying jobs, and those with the ability to work from home. Unfortunately, most African Americans belong to either the first or the second group. They are working low-paying jobs and cannot complete their work from home so; they have to go out of their homes, neglecting their safety, to earn a living for their families. Doctors recommend people boost their immune systems by eating nutrition-filled food that will help them develop the strength to fight the virus. Most African Americans cannot afford such healthy diets because of low wages. These low wages are one reason this virus has affected the black community the most in the United States. Evidence shows that black Americans obtain very little attention from their healthcare providers. For instance, in New York City, reports indicate there are more deaths of black people compared to the white community, who receive better and quicker treatments. Symptoms of black people are neglected until they reach a stage where they must breathe through ventilators, where they are left to fight alone.

Authorities issued social distancing and mandatory mask wearing rules, but many white people disobeyed those instructions, claiming that wearing a mask violates their right to freedom. By defying these rules, they not only put themselves at risk of being infected but also spreading the deadly virus among their family members and those whom they come in contact with. The armed militia also did not stay indoors. They marched in the streets and across this nation, protesting against the lockdown, even when they know that they can reduce the spread of the disease by staying home and practicing social distancing. People are starting to become careless, as they have started visiting parks and beaches without wearing proper facial masks. They are spreading COVID-19 faster, fully aware of the gravity of the situation. People need to see the videos of those who are dying, struggling to take a few breaths because of this lethal disease. If they saw these videos, then they might realize their mistake and start following rules implemented by the government. Together they can help prevent the spread of this disease.

People who complain about wearing facial masks because it troubles their breathing or makes them feel hot should understand that their actions do not affect only them but also their society. Not only the elderly but also children are dying because of the negligence of these adults. Many normally healthy people catch this virus and die because of the negligence of someone else. For instance, a bus driver told his passenger to wear a mask, but this passenger ignored his command. The bus driver died from the coronavirus some days later. If she had listened to him, he could still be with his family right now.

Why African Americans face this type of discrimination in the healthcare system is related to how the white community of the United States views people of color. Many healthcare professionals, for example, have served in their field and its people for years. Dr. Jocelyn Elders is one who comes to mind. She was appointed in 1993 by President Bill Clinton to serve as the first African American and the second woman to serve as Surgeon General of the United States.

Minority groups, such as African Americans and Hispanics, living in a white-dominant culture, have encountered serious consequences due to a poor healthcare system. Dangerous diseases such as cardiovascular diseases (CVDs), diabetes, and cancers are more prevalent among these groups than others. The reason is the same; they neither get proper healthcare services nor can pay for expensive health care services. The coronavirus has affected them in the same way. They have become more susceptible to this virus than white people. These groups can hardly get proper food three times a day, so where would they obtain money for their healthcare? President Barack Obama, on March 23, 2010, signed the Affordable Care Act into law. However, since that time, Republicans have tried to repeal this law over 63 times. Each time they chip away at the coverage, they endanger those with no health insurance. These repeals are why many African Americans and people of color have inadequate insurance coverage; therefore, they do not receive proper treatment for their illness and when they are hospitalize it usually too late and they end up dying looking for help. Several healthcare organizations work in the United States for the welfare of its people. Some of these organizations try their best to provide emergency healthcare services to white people. Although, when it comes to providing the same services to the black community, they turn their backs and neglect them as if they do not exist or are not United States citizens.

The African American community deserves equal rights, like any other community in the United

States. We should design strategies to ensure they acquire the same healthcare opportunities and treatment. All patients should be treated like human beings, not as an African American, Hispanic, or Caucasian. There are numerous examples in history where healthcare professionals treated their patients based on ethnic or racial groups. There are many laws to resolve such issues in the healthcare sector, but all have failed so far. The best way to end this discrimination would be to make changes in the healthcare system and provide patients the same services, regardless of their race. Harsh penalties should go to any healthcare professional that continues to treat patients of color differently.

People are more interested in gaining temporal things rather than making their characters stronger. An approach to exterminate racial differences in the healthcare sector is making people aware of their responsibilities toward humanity. Patients and workers should both learn to understand the differences among each other and work towards improvement without letting these interpersonal differences become a hindrance. They must learn that the planet is equally for all. It is the responsibility of higher power authorities to ensure that no sector of minorities are left behind to suffer alone just because they are low-income workers. With this stated, people will not suffer.

Most of the reported cases of COVID-19 are from the black community, which is the result of misdiagnosis and mistreatment that they have been enduring for years. Black people are more likely to be ignored or put on the waiting list of patients. Black people suffer at the hands of even their doctors, who take an oath to serve all patients the same, failing to do their jobs properly when they allow racial thoughts to dominate their minds. Doctors have been mistreating African Americans for years, and they are tired of the injustice.

A white person exhibiting symptoms of the disease would receive better care than minor groups who exhibit the same symptoms. We must formulate plans to ensure that this unfair treatment in the healthcare sector is changed so that everyone enjoys the same resources. People should be made aware of the effects of the ill-treatment it has on the black community, victimized mentally and physically. As governments have started to loosen lockdown restrictions, everyone needs to continue wearing facial masks, keep a distance of six feet, and avoid large gatherings so that they save their lives and the lives of others. These precautions will protect essential workers, who are mostly black people and will allow them to do their jobs without as much worry.

Now that we have brought healthcare discrimination to light, its effects on the physical and mental health of minorities, how laws could be improved, and new strategies, we could introduce to lessen this gap between the white and black communities. This racial discrimination will not affect black people alone; it will harm society as a whole. We should introduce proper evidence-based strategies with the power to show positive results for a better future and a better world.

CHAPTER 15
The Purpose Behind Taking A Knee

Racism in American has existed for centuries. White people enjoy the freedom of legal and social rights, while minorities cannot execute their rights and privileges because of their ethnicity or race. Over the years, many black Americans have protested against unequal civil rights, but the issue persists. Many people continue to fight and raise their voices on different platforms.

All over the world, people use gestures to articulate the purpose and objectives of their protests. Similarly, taking a knee is a gesture in which the protestors kneel to exhibit their desire for freedom from the oppression that black Americans face across the nation every day. This gesture was used on September 1, 2016, when Colin Kaepernick of the San Francisco 49ers took a knee during the national anthem to express his thoughts on police brutality and racism. He later stated at a press conference his true intention behind the protest, "I am not going to stand up to show pride in a flag for a country that oppresses black people and people of color." He further stated, "To me, this is bigger than football, and it would be selfish on my part to look the other way. There are bodies in the street and people getting paid leave and getting away with murder." Before taking a knee, Kaepernick protested by sitting on the bench on August 26, 2016, but this gesture did not get much recognition. Therefore, after taking the advice of former NFL player Nate Boyer, he took a knee at that later game, which people noticed immediately and reacted differently towards the gesture.

If we look back over history, we will come to know that this gesture has a long history as Dr. Martin Luther King Jr. and his fellow civil rights marchers first used it decades ago. On February 1, 1965, the leader of civil rights, Dr. King Jr., took a knee during a march over the voting rights of black Americans in Selma, Alabama. He took a knee for a group prayer before going to jail. The photo of him kneeling emerged after the NFL player protests. Since then, several NFL players have taken a knee during the American national anthem. For the same cause, many athletes have protested in different ways with different gestures.

After the death of George Floyd in Minneapolis, taking a knee has now become a symbol that represents anti-racism. This brutal act ignited a new fire, and many people protested using this pose to perform their solidarity with black people. In the United Kingdom on June 3, 2020, Stand Up To Racism, an organization that works to eradicate anti-racist activities, held a kneeling protest to show unity against the violation of the rights of black Americans. After this event, First Secretary of States and Secretary of Foreign and Commonwealth Affairs, Dominic Raab, gave an ignorant statement regarding the kneeling protests. He admitted that while he might not know the history of this pose, it looks like it is from the Game of Thrones series. He received heavy criticism for this embarrassing statement.

After Kaepernick's protest, many of his fans were offended and considered it disrespectful to the army and the American flag. However, the former United States president, Barack Obama, supported the action of the athlete, saying that he has a right to put forward his opinion about something worth considering. On the other hand, the current United States president, Donald Trump, has been very harsh regarding these protests. He saw this form of protest as very disrespectful. During a campaign stop in Alabama, Trump said, "Wouldn't you love to see one of these NFL owners, when somebody disrespects our flag, say, "Get that son of a bitch off the field right now. Out, He's fired. He's fired"."

After this flippant statement by President Trump, many NFL players chose not to come out on the game field, and other teams protested in their own way. Even players from other sports, such as basketball and baseball, joined in these protests. In 2018, officials created a new rule: players on the field during the national anthem must stand during the anthem, or else the team would receive a fine. This new rule did not stop athletes from standing against racism; many players continued their kneeling protests, regardless of the consequences.

Although Kaepernick was not treated fairly in his right to protest, he stood up for his values and principles without fearing the consequences. He sacrificed his football career and many endorsements, but nothing could force him to stop standing against the cruelty of police brutality. After starting this protest, he said, "If they take football away and my endorsements from me, I know that I stood up for what is right." Every time a new case of police brutality emerges, the picture of Kaepernick taking a knee becomes fresh, and people feel motivated to take a stand against what is wrong. In 2018, during its anniversary campaign, Nike made Colin Kaepernick the face of Just Do It, in which they wrote the tagline "Believe in something, even if it means sacrificing everything" on the advertisement including Kaepernick's face.

In 1968, Tommie Smith and John Carlos performed a Black Power Salute, raising their fisted right hand in the air and bowing their heads after winning and receiving their medals at the Summer Olympics. This salute was a sign of respect and a protest after the assassination of Dr. Martin Luther King Jr. They wanted to raise their voices to a global platform against the unjust treatment of black people and other minorities living in the United States. This form of protest caused their disqualification from the games, but they never regretted giving a voice to the people opposed.

Another example of protests by athletes is Mahmoud Abdul-Rauf, an NBA basketball player who refused to participate during the national anthem. He would not stand for a national anthem that represented brutality, injustice, and racism. He would either stay in the locker room during the anthem or raise his hands in prayer when he had to come on the floor for the national anthem. Yet another example is Muhammad Ali, a renowned athlete, who refused to join the Vietnam War. The government asked him to fight against Vietnam, but he refused. He did not see why he should stand against a country by going against his beliefs while joining hands with people who had never treated him like a human being. There are many examples of people who stood up for their beliefs and the right to protest without fear.

These protests will continue until, as a society, we provide justice and equal rights to black people and other minorities living in the United States. It is up to us to choose right from wrong. We all live with two choices. One choice is to be the knee that chokes others, silences their voices, and kills innocent people, while the other one is to be the knee that bows for what is right. Either you take a knee, or they will put a knee on your neck. Keeping in mind that what you sow, you shall reap. If we do not stand with the oppressed today, a time will come when we will face the same brutality in one way or another. We must take a stand against racism and brutality, not only for the rights of black people but also for the sake of all of humanity that is becoming endangered day by day at the hands of the oppressor.

CHAPTER 16

Say Their Names

The year 2020 has not been easy for anyone in the world. When the COVID-19 pandemic hit, it caused fear, uncertainty, an economic crisis, sickness, and death. The murder of George Floyd sparked rage and protests against racism and police brutality. The heart-wrenching video of his last minutes unveiled the true face of the judicial system who claim to be protectors of citizens, regardless of their race or color. Thousands of black people have died over the years at the hand of the police because of their skin color. In this nation and many others around the world where a person skin color can cost a person their life. There are three times more chances for black people to die in police encounters than white people. The black population is lower than the white is, but the ratio of black-to-white deaths by police is very high. In 2017, police killed 1129 people, out of which 25% were black people.

Tony McDade, Ahmaud Arbery, Sean Reed, Breonna Taylor, George Floyd: these are the names of people who have died because of police encounters in 2020. There are thousands of names that should also be remembered. Black Americans feel uncertainty and fear because of what happens in their community; this holds them back from stepping out of their homes. A person of any color should not spend their life in terror and panic. Justice without peace is impossible, so we cannot wait for the change to happen by itself. Instead, we are the ones who must bring change. We cannot watch more black Americans being shot or choked by racist's individuals. It is time to take a stand, to tell the world that the life of each black person matters. There is no other way to fight this deadly disease of racial hatred known as racism than to confront and abolish it. It is high time for black people to come forward and tell their daily experiences; of how they do not have the same opportunities and how the justice system has failed to provide justice for them. The people have woken up from a deep slumber of superiority and bias. They are willing to raise their voices against those institutions that endorse racism and take pride in being white. We must stand and condemn white supremacy and maltreatment while ensuring that violence and rage do not disturb the peace and the black community wins their rights on high and moral ground.

Listing the names of the black people killed by police can be exhausting. While few names have made headlines and social media campaigns, others remain unknown and hidden. The guilty police officers are punished or terminated in rare cases, but usually, they are left free to kill again. The need is to punish these criminals not only on paper but also in practice. Unless we change the mindset that being different is not scary or inferior, we cannot live in harmony. Children from an early age should learn to respect people of color, and the sense of inclusion should be in their hearts so that later, they do not discriminate against a black person or any person of color and become part of the toxic, racist system.

Now, whenever we hear the news of the death of a black person at the hand of white people, it looks familiar. The details are so similar that they have started to echo and intermingle with each other. The movement, Black Lives Matter, has helped point out the disproportionate murders of black people, by sending a message that people of all color, and race stand with the black community to fight this war on racism. The data cannot be relied upon to determine the exact number of killings, because police departments hide and protect their heinous acts by altering the numbers and do not report incidents not caught on camera.

Young people, the asset of society and source of help and comfort for parents, are to be protected and celebrated, but young black men are the main target of the police. Police arrest them for charges like street fights, curfew violations, drug possession, or dealing drugs, based on suspicion without allowing them the opportunity to speak on their defense. Tortures take place at police stations, and if they show resistance, killed on the spot. Likewise, black women when arrested because of petty crimes or because of their skin color are sexually and emotionally harass. Arrests happen at schools or colleges, where law enforcement officers discriminate between white and black students. Inappropriate touching while searching is common for black girls. Such treatment imprints long-lasting and severe issues of mental health of youngsters. Their confidence level drops and they feel isolated and frightened, ruining their chances of having a bright future and a successful career. Unless the families of murdered black people receive justice, this systematic racism will strengthen its roots deeper into society and continue to create havoc.

#SayTheirName is a social media hashtag used to keep the memories alive of those black people who lost their lives due to prejudice and racism. The campaign motivates people to mention or recognize those black people not as victims of racism, but as people who had distinct personalities and names. This campaign is a way to show solidarity with the families of the deceased, and remind their killers that those people were human beings and deserved to live their lives and aspire for a good future, just like any other human being. The #SayTheirName campaign boldly and repeatedly mentions the names so that they cannot go into oblivion without getting justice. The name of every victim demands attention and importance, and their names should be repeated repeatedly until higher authorities stop favoring white people and degrading black people.

Say Their Names:

Trayvon Martin:

Trayvon Martin was a 17-year-old unarmed black male from Miami Gardens, Florida. On February 26, 2012, he was fatally shot by George Zimmerman in Sanford, Florida. Martin had gone on a visit with his father to his father's fiancée at her townhouse in the Twin Lakes community in Sanford. On that dreadful evening of February 26, 2012, Martin was walking alone back to the fiancée's house from a nearby convenience store. Zimmerman, a member of the community watch, saw Martin and reported him as a suspicious figure to the Sanford Police Department. Several minutes later, there was an altercation, and Zimmerman fatally shot Martin in the chest. Zimmerman was eventually charged and put on trial, but the jury acquitted him of second-degree murder and manslaughter in July of 2013.

Alton Sterling:

Alton Sterling was a 37-year-old black man who was selling CDs and DVDs in a store when he was shot to death at close range by two racist white police officers, one of which was named Blane Salamoni. The two police officers were trying to arrest Sterling for possessing guns, which later was revealed by the shop owner that Sterling kept the guns due to the fear of robbery. He was first shot with an electric taser, then laid on his stomach on the ground, and finally shot six times. Even after shooting, Salamoni continued abusing him. Later, Salamoni lost his job, and the other officer received a suspension, but no charges one was charged.

Freddie Gray:

Freddie Gray was a 25-year-old black man, was arrested because of possession of a knife in 2015. A police van transported Gray, and after 45 minutes, was found dead due to excessive beatings and torture. His spinal cord was displaced from falling around inside the moving vehicle; he was handcuffed and wore no seatbelt. The government compensated the family with a monetary payout, and some police officers were charged while others were exonerated.

John Crawford:

John Crawford was a 22-year-old young man who went shopping at Walmart on August 5, 2014. He was shot to death by police for holding a BB gun, which did not belong to him but was on sale in the store. The police officer wrongly considered it a real gun and shot him two times on arm and torso. The jury chose not to file charges against the police officer.

Michael Brown:

An 18-year-old black boy, Michael Brown, was walking with his friend when he was brutally murdered after being shot 12 times by a police officer in 2014. The police officer, Darren Wilson, while sitting in his car, grabbed Brown by his neck, and threatened him. When he showed resistance, the officer shot him. Later, Wilson accused the deceased boy of attacking him, but eyewitnesses and Brown's friend claimed the opposite. Wilson never was charged for murder, which was heavily criticized by the media and sparked protests.

Jordan Davis:

Jordan Davis was a 17-year-old student who was murdered by a software developer, Michael David Dunn. The shooting took place in November of 2012 at a gas station. Dunn got infuriated because of loud music playing in the car that Davis and his two friends sat in while a third friend was in the store. The argument became heated and led to a gunshot, resulting in the death of Davis. Dunn shot Davis in the legs, aorta, and stomach. Dunn immediately ran from the spot, but later testified to committing murder and was charged.

Sandra Bland:

Twenty-eight-year-old African American female, Sandra Bland, was arrested and tased on July 10, 2015, on a minor traffic violation. Three days later, she was found hanged in her cell. Her death was ruled as a suicide by the police staff. Her death also ignited protests, condemning her arrest for a crime that was insignificant and demanded an investigation into whether she died due to suicide or murder. The police officer who arrested her received temporary leave for poor handling of traffic stop rules instead of proper punishment. This incident reveals that black people are arrested for petty crimes more than white people.

Botham Jean:

An innocent 26-year-old black man, Botham Jean, was sitting on his sofa eating ice cream in the safety of his home when an off-duty patrol officer barged in and shot him to death. Officer Guyger mistakenly believed that this was her apartment, and a thief had entered into her home. This incident also sparked rage and protests. Guyger was sentenced to 10 years of imprisonment by the court for killing an unarmed person.

Oscar Grant:

Oscar Grant was a 22-year-old African American who was force to lay on the ground on his stomach before being shot to death in the back on New Year's Eve in 2009. The Bay Area Rapid Transit

Police Department (BART) received a report of a fight on a train. Police officers responded and held up some passengers, including Oscar Grant. A police officer kneeled on his head and forcefully put him on the ground face down while another officer shot him in the back. Grant was taken to the hospital but later died. The officer who shot him was found guilty of manslaughter.

Corey Jones:

Corey Jones was a 31-year-old African American who was standing beside his disabled car when he was shot dead by police officer Nouman K Raja. The officer was in plain clothes when he approached Jones and fired six times. During an investigation, he gave a false statement that he shot in self-defense, but he was caught in his lies by an audio recording. Raja was found guilty of manslaughter and negligence.

Ahmaud Arbery:

Another incident of racism was when a 25-year-old African-American, Ahmaud Arbery, was shot to death while jogging. Three white men followed him; two of them were father and son, and both of them had weapons. Travis McMichael and his father ignited a confrontation and arguments, followed by the murder of Arbery. Until a video was released, there was a deliberate delay in the arrests. This delay aroused rage in protestors, and the justice system of the United States started to receive questions. Later, under pressure from protesters, the murderers were charged.

Breonna Taylor:

Another tragic story was that of a 26-year-old African American female who was an emergency medical technician. While she slept in her bed on March 13, 2020, three civilian-clothed Louisville Metro Police Department (LMPD) officers, executing a no-knock search warrant, entered her apartment in Louisville, Kentucky. Kenneth Walker, Taylor's boyfriend, shot and wounded one of the officers, which he thought were home intruders. When the police returned fire, they fatally shot Taylor. The officers claimed that they were searching for suspects as part of a drug investigation when this fatal event took place.

George Floyd:

The recent murder of George Floyd on May 25, 2020, caused worldwide debate and sparked protests, demanding justice for the black community and reviving the Black Lives Matter movement. This death will go down in the history of America. George Floyd was a 46-year-old black American who was killed by a Minneapolis police officer. He was allegedly, charged with using counterfeit money to buy cigarettes. One of the officers of the arrest, Derek Chauvin, put his knee on the neck of Floyd for eight straight minutes and forty-six seconds until he choked to death. The video of the incident circulated the internet and caused a storm. The officer eventually was charged with first-degree murder.

Jacob Blake:

On August 23, 2020, a 29-year-old African-American man was shot and paralyzed by police officer Rusten Sheskey in Kenosha, Wisconsin. Four of seven shots fired at his back during an arrest by the officers hit him. Three of Blake's sons were in the backseat. Attorney General Josh Kaul later said that police found a knife on the floor of the vehicle, though he would not describe it or say whether it was related to the shooting; Jacob's lawyers said that the knife was not in Jacob's possession.

CHAPTER 17

"No One Is Going To Save Us, But Us"

The citizens of the United States have the power to use their voices to create changes against racial discrimination. Racism has affected African Americans by causing them to be brutalize and lose their lives, yet little action has happened to eradicate the challenges that African Americans have faced for decades. Mothers fear for their sons because they do not know if they will be the next victim of brutality. While many people seek answers as to why the attitude toward African Americans is so disturbing, there is a lot more that the citizens of the United States could do to change this type of mindset and improve the lives of the affected population.

Racism refers to the different traits that people use to show a level of superiority over other races. When a certain group of people feels superior to others and uses all types of form of harsh and degrading tactics even murder to ensure this superiority, which is racism. People have always used the biological differences of people to indicate hierarchy in society. This hierarchy has led to some groups receiving better treatment than others do. Because of this, I believe that racism will always exist, and it is upon people to learn how to accommodate each other and do away with oppressions and hostilities that comes with racism.

Racism is a behavior or reaction that Americans can end through education. Education is the key when it comes to the deconstruction of all forms of racial narratives. Americans have, for many years, engaged in debates on how they can stop racism, but still, a portion of the population has not come to terms with these ideas. The most affected, in this case, are African Americans who try to live their lives conductively with the rest of the population.

Leaders do very little when it comes to addressing racism. For instance, the current president of the United States, Donald Trump, has mostly remained silent on the issue, only arguing that a strong economy is the best antidote. The president must learn to understand that people cannot build the economy when people live in fear. Families become unproductive because of the misery that comes with losing a loved one, especially under avoidable circumstances. As such, President Trump claims that he has done more for the black community in comparison to past presidents, such as Abraham Lincoln. The issue of economic stability cannot address the issue of racism. Leaders must identify the best approaches to resolve existing gaps to end racism.

The current president is divisive on the issue of racism because, at times, he uses words that intimidate and humiliate African Americans and immigrants. President Trump is an example of a leader who believes that unless people rise to advocate or change, he will not make amendments to protect the rights of minorities. We must utilize education as a means to teach our younger generations the importance of interacting with others outside of their race. A diverse education effectively helps alleviate the proliferation of discriminatory discourses to promote intercultural connections. Classes about different cultures must be required in the United States. These classes will ensure that both white and black children are in classes together, and they will receive the same kind of education on cultural values and differences.

According to a report published by the Associated Press (2020), Atlanta Mayor, Keisha Lance, indicated that the "silence on racism and harsh rhetoric toward protesters have created a confounding dynamic for a consequential national conversation."

Similarly, in a report published by Fowler (2020), in Fox News, it is evident that slavery is an issue of the past but racial double standards continue to affect both the police departments and the courtrooms, and the environment of learning. These issues originate from racism and the absence of available equal opportunities.

In classes, students should learn that racism is not only about skin color but also about cases of discrimination on individuals who are culturally or physically different. White people have, for many years, felt that black people have a physique that connects them to crime and, therefore, causes problems in society. However, many have not realized that this form of racism is also an act of stereotyping. Using a small group of people to generalize a whole is an act of racism that students should learn.

Education will help reduce racism when students learn about racist tendencies. The most common racist tendencies are those that involve prejudice and discrimination against people of color. When students learn about these tendencies, they will realize that what is happening is unethical and, therefore, they will find a way to stop it. Awareness is one of the best ways to deal with racism, with education being the basis of it all.

Education will also open the eyes of America to the historical racist issues and effects. For many years, African Americans was the subject of slavery. During the 18th and 19th centuries, there were many cases of slavery and human trafficking. African Americans were the victims of these and other inhumane acts and, therefore, end up engaged in riots to end them. One slave revolt that stands out was by Nat Turner who led the only effective, sustained slave rebellion (August 1831) in U.S. history. Turner believing in signs and hearing divine voices, He was convinced by a solar eclipse of the sun that the time was right to rise up, and he enlisted the help of other enslaved men in the area but later the insurrection ended with all of the participants being killed with Nat Turner being hanged. The negative impacts when taught in a class that has a mixture of blacks and whites, will bring enlightenment to the subject to help reduce racial tension. Understanding the negative impacts of racism helps, many realize the importance of unity and, therefore, avoid issues based on skin color.

Eliminating racism calls for education on diversity and practicing it in all aspects. The American workplace has always faced problems associated with racism some people have made efforts to educate employees and their employers about diversity, inclusivity, and multicultural aspects, marred when racist comments persist in the workplace. To end racism, the workplace needs to be well prepared to engage in discussions on the impacts of discrimination and stereotyping. There is no progress if employees in the workplace are not aware of the influence of racism and decisions made in that aspect.

Education on diversity is effective if it is done practically; by ensuring that people volunteer in multicultural groups. For instance, groups made up of African Americans who are engaging in social activities, should also incorporate white people. A multicultural group like this will make the members realize each other's potential and forget about racism. Volunteering is part of accepting the fact that different races make a society, and that means accommodating each other leads to unity and harmony.

The American government should also come up with an effective initiative that ensures people join an after-school cultural group. The group should have people of different races and cultural backgrounds to incorporate their differences. The compulsory requirement of joining these after-school cultural groups will ensure that black and white people mingle as a means of doing away with the differences they endure. Friendships and relationships developed out of groups, and this helps clear out the idea of racial differences among the members.

Racism could also end by educating people on how to cope and interact with people of different races. Education of this kind should start at the elementary level. Children should learn how to mingle with other children of different races while young so that they can grow without the perception of discrimination, prejudice, or stereotypes.

The early stages of life should involve educating the young about the importance of equality and unity. This early education should promote intercultural interactions and the embracement of diversity. When a child realizes that he or she is of a different race and that there are others of the same kind, then they should refrain from any form of racial discrimination. They tend to feel that the color differences that they bear do not create any difference in terms of their performance in class or the opportunities that they have in life. The friends that they have should, therefore, be of different races. Therefore, this form of education should begin during the early stages of life.

The government should take part in this process by educating the people on how to be vocal about racial issues. Educational institutions must learn how to help people understand how to speak up when faced with racism or discrimination. This understanding will happen after carefully explaining the impacts of racism on society in a profound way. These impacts will help society refrain from being quiet about critical matters that pertains to racial issues.

Pushing people to be vocal about racial issues and pointing them out will bring attention on racial issues. Many fear that they will be attacked if they speak up about racism. Many people have been silenced and even assassinated for being vocal about racism. The government should be stricter when coming up with policies that deter Americans from subjecting African Americans or people of color from racist reactions and comments.

All of these activities revolve around education and awareness of the negative effects of racism. Learning how to communicate openly and developing the art of understanding will help eliminate racism. The higher educational institutions should ensure that each student learns how to communicate without stereotypes and understand the differences that exist between them.

America has discriminated against people of color because they have not received proper education on the negative impacts of such acts. Besides, they do not mingle or interact with people of different cultures to understand the importance of diversity. Educating people has proved to be the most effective way of ending racism and bringing people to together for the common good of all humanity.

CHAPTER 18

Will Reparations Be Enough?

America is home to millions of people belonging to different races and nationalities, but it also harbors racial hostility against non-white people. The recent deaths of George Floyd, Ahmaud Arbery, and other countless unreported cases of brutality speak for themselves that America is not a safe for people of color. The prejudice and racist behavior in every sector, whether it is educational, professional, or political are obvious and hostile towards black people. Despite contributing to society with sincerity and hard work for centuries, black people are still considered outsiders and, infact, non-human beings. Although the United States Constitution was created to guarantee freedom to all its citizens but black people, still do not have the right to life, success, and other basic rights.

The origin of racism can be trace back to slavery, which is the most offensive sin of the United States of America. Even the Civil War and the Emancipation Proclamation could not absolve America of this sin. During the 17th and 18th centuries, thousands of Africans were abducted from their homelands and forcefully imported to America and its colonies for cheap, hard manual labor. They received inhumane treatment, compelled to do such tasks that white people thought were too inferior and degrading for them. Africans used to do hard labor under harsh and severe conditions, risking their lives. White slave masters deliberately kept them away from reading and writing, dictating their every action like puppets. After years of sexual, emotional, psychological, and economic exploitation, because of the Civil War, slavery was abolished. Amendments to the United States Constitution granted black people the right to citizenship, to vote, and to equal treatment and protection under the law. However, even lawmakers often ignore these amendments. The abolishment of slavery had finally happened, but its roots have grown into more hideous and ugly forms of slavery called systemic racism. The biased behavior at schools, colleges, workplaces, and public places is one way of showing hatred and contempt towards black people. When Dr. Martin Luther King, Jr. told the American nation about his dream, his eyes filled with hope for black people of America, that one day they will be entirely free from the chains of slavery and racism. He dreamed of creating an America where everyone could live fearlessly and respectfully without worrying about oppression or exploitation. However, his dream remains only a dream for black people, which does not seem to be turning into reality anytime soon. African Americans escaped slavery after a hard struggle and many sacrifices, but this ghost of racism continues to haunt them, making millions of black people victims.

The American dream foretells that by focusing on goals and working hard to achieve them, any person can live a content life with a house, business, and other comforts that they own. However, the United States government policies make this dream impossible for black Americans. In the 1860s, cheap labor and production helped the United States economy boom, making the white slave masters rich through economic exploitation of their black slaves. Several movements and public demonstrations have demanded reparations for more than 400 years of slavery, brutality, lynching, murders, and exploitation. There have been debates on how black people should receive compensation for all the wrongdoings done to them.

Reparations are compensation given to someone abused or injured, usually in the form of money. Giving out these reparations are not unknown to American history. When people must leave their houses or other areas for some developmental purpose, they receive compensation in the form of money or land. The government gives reparations to the families of soldiers who die in wars. The United States launched the Marshal Plan as reparation to help the Jewish community affected by the holocaust. Black people still have not received reparations for the brutality they received during slavery, which hoarded the wealth for white families. In their travels from Africa to America, 15% of slaves died due to unfavorable traveling conditions. Many black women were sexually assaulted, families were divided, and slaves were lynched, beaten, and exploited. After the Civil War, each black family was promised 40 acres and a mule as reparation. However, after the assassination of Abraham Lincoln, the lands were returned to slave owners, which, in turn, forced black slaves back to their white masters. During the Great Depression, those policies were adopted, which lifted white families while ignoring the black community. Reparation is a promise that was never fulfilled by the United States government. Many suggestions have been made on how reparations should be made, but no decisions have been reached as of yet.

In 1894, a bill was approved in the Senate, which promised cash payments and monthly pensions to the former slaves, but with the start of World War I, the bill was forgotten. In 1969, James Forman asked for reparations from churches and synagogues for endorsing slavery. In 1980, some successful recompense on the order of the Supreme Court was made when the federal government paid reparations to eight Indian tribes for illegally annexing tribal land. In 1986, a movement started to force the government to provide educational funds for black students. Both white and black politicians have proposed many bills since then, but can this money or land compensate for the psychological, physical, and emotional trauma endured by black people for more than four centuries? Black slaves were separated from their families when taken from Africa and forced to leave their country to become slaves in American. They could not hold property or wealth for their families or future generations. These restrictions have caused the poverty and miserable conditions faced by black people today.

No amount of money could ever compensate 400 years of brutality, inhumane conditions, or murder. Asking for reparation is like equating life for a few dollars. Not even all the riches of the world could remove the days of imprisonment and inhumane working conditions for the innocent black people or soothe the pain of a mother whose son or daughter died because he or she looked suspicious in the eyes of a racist. Black people do not want reparations;

they want complete abolishment of racism so that they can live peacefully. They want a society where their children can be safe, where they can send them out to school or play without the fear of murder and humiliation. They want a place where police provide protection and serve them instead of killing them because of suspicious based on their skin color. Reparation is useless if the families of those killed by racists do not receive justice. The best reparation for black people is equality, respect, and justice. The other suggested reparations cannot repair the physical, psychological, and financial damage inflicted on black people since their arrival in America. Money cannot bring back the happiness of black families who have lost their fathers, brothers, or sons; it cannot cure the trauma faced by black children when they see and feel hatred and contempt around them.

The white slave masters who treated black slaves in the most brutal manner and black ancestors who endured hardships of that time are no longer alive, so the question arises; what should the reparation be? If the black descendants receive cash or pension, it will affect their sense of hard work and independence. This compensation will make them dependent on the government and taxpayers to fulfill their basic needs. This dependency will further alienate black people from white people. The system of collecting money from white people in the form of tax money ignites the feelings of superiority and hatred in the hearts of white people when many of them are not even racist and do not belong to the generations of white masters.

The only reasonable and appropriate solution of reparations is equality, justice, and respect. Black people want equal treatment so that they no longer feel like outsiders. They need love, peace, respect, and opportunities like the other people around them. Black parents want their children to have a quality education, health care, food, and chances of success. They no longer want their safety to feel threatened when they send their children outside the house. Black youngsters wish to excel in their studies and careers without prejudice by their teachers, colleague, or employers. Black children want to become friends with the children of their white neighbor's but cannot do so because they are considered a bad influence by the white parents.

Giving reparations to black people is similar to returning money robbed from black ancestors during slavery time. Black people worked hard on farms and plantations, but in return, they received nothing but hatred.

The need now is to change the situation and the mindset of racist people. The loss of lives and respect, emotional stability cannot be atoned by a few dollars. After the abolishment of slavery, black people should have received compensation immediately so that they could save themselves from generations of racism and poverty. It is never too late, although, the only possible reparation now is to open the doors of all opportunities for black people and introduce new bills to take action against police departments that arrest and kill innocent black people. The need is to make the black community feel secured and safe where no Mother is afraid to send their children out the door and wonder if they will return home safe and secure. African Americans want opportunities where they can be free to choose their destiny and have a bright future for their children.

CHAPTER 19

We the People: Broken Promises

The Constitution of the United States went into effect on March 4, 1789 and remains active, even after surviving more than 200 years. It consists of seven articles in total. In them, separation of power between states and the federal government, and the federal government three main branches: Legislative, Judicial, and Executive Branches, are described. The government was structured to have some limitations to protect the basic rights of people.

So far, around 27 amendments have been made in the United States Constitution. Many of them were for the protection or provision of equal human rights of the citizens, but have those amendments been effective? Have the amendments, or the Constitution itself, brought any benefit to the more than 42 million black Americans who have struggled against racial discrimination for years? Have they received equal rights not only on paper but in real life as well?

In 1787, Gouverneur Morris, one of the Founding Fathers of the United States, used the term, We the People, to describe all Americans living in the country while he was giving the Constitution final touches. He used these powerful words in the Preamble of the United States Constitution, which describes what is in the rest of the Constitution. The Preamble is famous for its first 52 words that read as:

> "We the People of the United States, in Order to form a more perfect Union, establish Justice, ensure domestic Tranquility, provide for the common defense, promote the general Welfare, and secure the Blessings of Liberty to ourselves and our Posterity, do ordain and establish this Constitution for the United States of America."

The three words at the start of the Constitution have great power. These words show who has power in the United States. They show that the Constitution does not give all the power to a king or a president, but it is the people who rule the country, who protect each other's rights, who try to make their society better than yesterday. The word we in We the people is not only for white men and for women, but it is for every single person who is an American citizen, no matter a person's class, race, or background.

There was no mention of slavery or race introduced in the Constitution at that time. In the Constitution, the rulebook, everybody was included in this use of We, irrespective of his or her skin color. This document promised the provision of equal respect, rights, opportunities, and protection, but were these promises kept, or did they just stay a part of the rulebook? Why is it that black people continue to fight for equal rights and opportunities?

In 1865, the 13th amendment to the United States Constitution ended slavery in all states, but with the end of slavery birthed a new era of racism and brutality. White people considered themselves superior and were not ready to provide equal opportunities to black people, especially in the southern states. After three years, in 1868, the 14th amendment to the United States Constitution was created, which granted citizenship to any person who was born in the United States, no matter their race or background. This amendment also promised the provision of equal security to all.

The government added the 15th amendment in 1870, which gave the right to vote to all Americans, no matter their status or race. These amendments show that promises of equality for black people were made, but the Constitution remained infected with the germs of racism. The Confederate States Constitution was created in 1861 and remained active for one whole year. This document used terms like Negro slaves many times throughout to deny black people equal rights.

Although the creation of these amendments favored black people, after so many years, they have failed to keep their promises. The rights of black people had been suppressed in these states and the law fail to protect them. In 1883, The Supreme Court denied the Civil Rights Act, which was passed in 1875, which gave many states a chance to treat black people with brutality.

This act of the Supreme Court forced many black people to move to the North to protect themselves. Although, white people never stopped humiliating them to show their superiority in every opportunity. Reconstruction in 1865-1877 brought changes in the history of black people. Many white racists could not accept these changes, so they created the Jim Crow Laws in the South, which took racial discrimination at the next level.

According to these laws, black people could not attend the same schools as white people, could not enjoy the same public facilities or services. The injustice of these laws has not stopped to date. The laws of the United States should have protected all humans equally, but they never fulfilled their promises. Many movements have fought for the rights of black people under the leadership of great personalities. Their efforts have helped black Americans get many rights, but still not equal to white Americans.

For instance, when the black people had enough of the cruelty, the Civil Rights Movements started in the 1950s, in which people protested in peaceful manners to raise their voice against injustice and inequality. Rather than hearing their demands and working with them for change, they were beaten, firehoses turn on them, along with vicious dogs, put in jails, and punished in other ways. This was done to discourage and suppress their voices from demanding equality. Black people who take a stand for their rights, for their protection, still die in the streets of a racist society.

The recent murder of George Floyd by the police is not something new in the United States history. Murders like this have happened for centuries in a society where the lives of black people do not matter or do not hold the same importance as the lives of white people. If we look back to the extreme act of brutality that happened in 1899 when Sam Hose was tortured for killing his employer in self-defense, we come to know that such murders and acts of injustice still exist in this society.

Even after centuries, the disease of racism from a racist society has not withdrawn. According to statistics, the police in the United States, which have the duty to protect and serve people no matter which race, has killed more black people than white people. Laws meant to protect people have become the cause of their death. We the People never fulfilled its promise of creating a tolerant and respectful society that is free of racism and full of harmony and fairness.

Black people still voice the unheard innocents who have died by the hand of law enforcement for no reason. To date, many black people have sacrificed their lives in the name of justice. Many continue to fight for the provision of equal opportunities. Sam Hose, Breonna Taylor, George Floyd, Sheku Bayoh, Kadiatou Diallo are just a few names of those who had committed the crime of having black skin in a society dominated by white people. They died by the system that had promised to protect their lives.

In the 21st century, where the United States has developed many new technologies and considered one of the great powers of the world, people living in its states still lose their lives at the hands of racist's individuals. The states have towering buildings and businesses running, yet they fail to provide justice to those who have demanded it for centuries. This nation has many great scientists making new scientific discoveries each day, yet its system has failed to eradicate the germs of racism from our society.

On one hand, "We the People" say that it will create a society near to perfection; while on the other hand; its system has never acknowledged the voices of those who demanded justice and equality. Eventually, a racist society will end. If the people who seek justice will continue to seek justice until they receive what they have struggled to have. Their voices cannot be silence. There will be no more sacrifices. They will continue rising and demanding their rights and freedom until they receive equal opportunities in society without facing racial discrimination.

A time will come when the dreams of black people will be valued and given an equal chance to shine in a society without any fear. A time will come when "I Have a Dream" by Dr. Martin Luther King, Jr. will come true. His words will transform themselves into reality. All the sacrifices and struggles, black people have made over the years will not be in vain; rather they will have the acknowledgment from none other than the system that failed them itself.

CHAPTER 20

A Time for Change

So far, we have brought to light the countless atrocities faced by black people and people of color as to how a political, educational, and social system discriminates against them on a daily basis. Contrary to public opinion, racial discrimination still exists, and black people have to face disrespect and humiliation daily. The police, which is supposed to serve and protect all citizens, nonetheless black people are beaten and arrested more often compared to white people. The fear of a black person in a white community is the reason for suspicion and discrimination. Racists use white fear to justify racist policies to make life more difficult for black people. The black community is more often associated with criminal activity, murders, drug use, and robbery. These are labels, which black people carry on themselves without given the opportunity to prove their innocence.

The United States law enforcement hands are stained with the blood of black people and other groups of minorities. There are jails and prisons which are overcrowded with black people, among whom most are innocent and serving time because of their skin color. Police are five times more likely to stop and search a black person than a white person. Black children face prejudice and mockery by their white classmates and teachers. Black women are exploited sexually and mentally. Due to poverty, they must take full-time jobs as domestic workers at low wages. This kind of oppression robs them of the opportunity to get an education, to progress, and their right to freedom.

Nevertheless, the United States is not the only victim of racism; it permeates every nook and corner of the world. Therefore, the effort to destroy the roots of racism should be global. Racism is the result of thinking that one race is biologically, physically, culturally, and mentally superior to other races. European imperialists have used this view to justify their colonial and racist policies. This sense of superiority has caused havoc around the world since ancient times when tribes waged wars to exert their power and dominance on other tribes. This same sense led the white Europeans to colonize around the world and introduce the concept of slavery in the country of America and other parts of the world. This sense of superiority and arrogance caused the holocaust by German Nazis. To justify the claim that Aryans were the purest race, they killed millions of people. They killed not only Jews, but also Africans and Romani people, and those that they considered useless and unworthy, such as people who were disabled, blind, deaf, homosexual, etc. It is ironic that America, which stood side by side with Allied forces to fight Nazism, was depriving the black community of their basic rights in America. Black people received universal voting rights in the 1960s, but the culture of systematic racism is still active.

White racists largely dominate the consumer market, manufacture products, and market them in a way that promotes the white people's lifestyles. Dark skin color is associated with ugliness and low living, while fair and light skin color symbolizes beauty and high-class status. Brands and companies subtly promote and endorse beauty concepts in which the fair skin is the standard. Advertisements of whitening cream depict the color black as the opposite of beauty and should lighten with their products; otherwise, society will not accept it. Girls and women are the victims of these so-called beauty standards that crush their self-confidence and self-esteem.

The death of George Floyd sparked anger and outrage worldwide, not only in the black communities, but people of all races took to the streets voicing their anger and frustration. The incident finally awakened the consciences of people who now are on the streets demanding justice for black people and willing to keep aside all racial differences and fight for the unity of humanity. We are working to remove the statues that somehow promote or symbolize racism and colonialism. The TV shows or movies that endorse racism and discrimination are being banned. People are speaking out about their painful experiences of racial injustice. All these protests have compelled the United States Congress to pass a bill to curb discretionary powers of the police. These actions mean that there is hope that racism will eventually vanish from the face of the earth if we take proactive steps against it collectively. The present chaos demands unity and peace, not discrimination or conflict. If we continue to judge people base on race, then the situation will worsen to the point of irreversible damage.

We should curb discrimination and racism on both individual and collective levels. When a person discriminates against their black neighbor, then on what moral ground can they fight and speak against universal racism? The need is to change the thinking that no one is better than another. The day we start to treat other people with the respect, dignity, kindness, and love that we want others to treat us, is the day that the menace of racism will begin to vanish. Unity and the equality of humanity are very important to fight against global issues. At the collective level, we should take part in eradicating systematic racism. For example, in schools, workplaces, and corporate level, black people should combine their voices to highlight the cruelty and monopoly used against them by white people. The politicians that use and create racist remarks and policies should not be elected to public office. The government should make inclusive policies, which benefit people of all race, and nationality.

Institutionalized racism is deeply rooted in our system and hard to dismantle, but not impossible. White people contribute to this racism, sometimes without even realizing it. Therefore, the need is to unfold the complex structure so that white people can also help in this struggle. They must stop using white privilege for obtaining favors or benefits, but while also raising their voices to dismantle this system of the white card. Children from a young age should learn about equality, antiracism, and respect for every person, whatever his or her race or origin. Our children will one day be the leaders of the future. Therefore, they should be tolerant and admirers of differences. Increasing the ratio of black people in arts, sports, culture, politics, media, business, and educational institutions will send a message to racist individuals that the majority wants a multi-ethnic world where we appreciate and celebrate diversity without favoring one race over another.

We know that we need the actions of both men and women to end gender inequality. In the same way, we require the participation of all races to end racism. This conflict would be less effective if black people fought alone for their rights because nobody would listen to them. The government and institutions would be pressured if white people march on the streets, demanding justice not for themselves but oppressed communities. The government will feel the urge to control the situation by holding those responsible for the unequal treatment accountable. The protesters are pressuring the criminal justice system to suspend the police officer who kneeled on the neck of George Floyd. Before him, all the guilty police officers escaped punishment or received temporary suspension to avoid the legal process.

Any kind of issue requires a deep understanding of the matter to find the solutions. Therefore, the need is to arrange seminars at schools and universities to educate students to report any form of racism. The students should be encouraged to ask open-ended questions so that no aspect is left unanswered. Communities should arrange meetings to address and find possible solutions for the betterment and improvement of oppressed people.

The anthropologist Franz Boas challenged eurocentrism, arguing that no culture is absolute or perfect. All culture is relative and should be judged only by context. He stated that we should all respect and celebrate differences and not disdain or ridicule them. Every culture of the world is beautiful and sacred for the respective people. Therefore, calling another culture useless, barbaric, or uncivilized hurts the feelings of the people following that culture. We should be flexible enough to tolerate different religions, cultures, norms, rituals, etc. because this makes the world diverse and colorful.

There are still people who want to create anarchy, hatred, and violence; they exist to build walls instead of bridges. These racist individuals keep hate of differences to exert their superiority on black people and people of color so that they cannot exceed white people in their field. Despite the current situation of hatred and negativity, we should not lose hope because the success and support of the protesters for the Black Lives Matter movement depict that peace-loving people outnumber racists and violent people. People are hopeful and determined to eradicate racism no matter what country, race, or color they belong too. No one but us can change the world; no supernatural force is going to come from another planet to save us from this global mayhem. Only together can we fight this invisible but deadly and powerful enemy. The Late Dr. Martin Luther King, Jr. said "Change does not roll in on the wheels of inevitability, but comes through continuous struggle. And so we must straighten our backs and work for our freedom. A man can't ride you unless your back is bent."

A survey asked how long it could take to curb racism. Four out of five responded that it could happen in 25 to 50 years. The loss of George Floyd and other black people should not go in vain. This death should be the start of hope and light for equality and unity. His story should be a turning point in this battle against racism. Now is the best time to remind the world that slavery ended centuries ago, so why basic human rights are still being denied to black people? Change can come, but it is up to each of us to do our part to bring awareness, which can bring an end to racism and encouraged peace, unity, and love. The future of humanity depends on us, and what we do now, we can no longer sit idly by and do nothing. Former President Barack H.

Obama said, "Change will not come if we wait for some other person or some other time. We are the ones we've been waiting for. We are the change that we seek." Now is the time that we take a stand and say no to racism.

Bibliography

Anderson, Carol. "In America, Black Deaths Are Not A Flaw In The System. They Are The System". The Guardian, Last modified 2020. https://www.theguardian.com/commentisfree/2020/jun/03/america-black-deaths-racism.

Edwards, Frank, Hedwig Lee, and Michael Esposito. "Risk Of Being Killed By Police Use Of Force In The United States By Age, Race–Ethnicity, And Sex". *Proceedings Of The National Academy*

Of Sciences 116, no. 34 (2019): 16793-16798. doi:10.1073/pnas.1821204116.

Hanna, Jason. "3 Recordings. 3 Cries Of 'I Can't Breathe.' 3 Black Men Dead After Interactions With Police". CNN, Last modified 2020. https://edition.cnn.com/2020/06/10/us/cant-breathe-deaths-javier-ambler-george-floyd-manuel-ellis/index.html.

He called police himself because of the panic attack due to the methamphetamine use.

https://www.usatoday.com/in-depth/news/investigations/2020/06/13/george-floyd-not-alone-dozens-said-cant-breathe-police-holds/3137373001/

https://edition.cnn.com/2020/06/01/business/black-ceos-george-floyd/index.html

Associated Press. "Race And Racism Go Largely Unaddressed In Trump Comments Since George Floyd'S Death". Marketwatch, Last modified 2020. https://www.marketwatch.com/story/race-and-racism-go-largely-unaddressed-in-trump-comments-since-george-floyds-death-2020-06-09.

Fowler, Richard. "Richard Fowler: After George Floyd Death, Trump Divides Americans Instead Of Uniting Us Against Racism". Fox News, Last modified 2020. https://www.foxnews.com/opinion/george-floyd-trump-richard-fowler.

Lartey, Jamiles, and Sam Morris. "How White Americans Used Lynchings To Terrorize And Control Black People". The Guardian, Last modified 2020. https://www.theguardian.com/

us-news/2018/apr/26/lynchings-memorial-us-south-montgomery-alabama.

Jodi L. Linley, "Racism Here, Racism There, Racism Everywhere: The Racial Realities Of Minoritized Peer Socialization Agents At A Historically White Institution", *Journal Of College Student Development* 59, no. 1 (2018): 21-36, doi:10.1353/csd.2018.0002.

History.com Editors, Nathanial "Nat" Turner (1800-1831) was an enslaved man who led a rebellion of enslaved people on August 21, 1831. https://www.history.com/topics/black-history/nat-turner

About The Author

Having a dream to rebuild decaying communities and lives by making the world a better place for all of humanity to live in peace and harmony, the Rev. Dr. Christopher D. Handy strives to raise the conscience of people everywhere to make a difference. His meager beginnings in a small rural town in Monroe, Louisiana, and his childhood in a housing project greatly contributed to his mission to enlighten, inform, educate, and motivate people to better themselves, their communities, and the world around them.

Dr. Handy has written many articles for various newspapers and magazines. He has organized marches to combat violence, injustices, poverty, and while in school in Michigan, he ministered on the 'bad' streets of Detroit and other cities. He continues to uphold justice and freedom by sharing his experiences with audiences everywhere. His first book, "The Scars of Racism" and his recent book "Racism: The Absence of Good", have made a stunning and positive impact on people of all races.

In 1999, Dr. Handy founded a non-denomination Christian Community Church Ministry called The New Testament Bible Church, and a non-profit organization called I.C.A.N (Innovative Community Action Network). Dr. Handy's focus is on the future of our younger generation and the outcasts of our society. Dr. Handy has developed a program called

ABOUT THE AUTHOR

"Christian Manhood Training Program" (CMTP), which is a rite of passage program, which deals with many of today's tough issues. Such as developing a relationship with God, treatment of women, the responsibility of being a Father, learning to love and not Kill, the importance of education, handling racism, and the dangers of drugs and alcohol abuse.

Dr. Handy is currently the CEO/President/Executive Director of Innovative Community Action Network (I.C.A.N.). His focus is working with at-risk and troubled youths, the poor and needy, the disenfranchised, and those without hope within the community by helping them to believe in themselves and encouraging them to strive for success. In 2002 he was honored with an Honorary Doctorate of Humanities Degree from The Institute of Christian Works for his work with his Mentoring Program for at-risk and troubled youths. Dr. Handy is also a certified prison fellowship counselor. He has spoken to numerous inmates of all ages on how to survive on the inside thus, preparing them for their release into society. Dr. Handy is a Licensed and Certified Counselor/Certified Life skills Coach and Trainer/Adult Organizational Development Specialist. Dr. Handy is a Certified Private Postsecondary Educator in Christian Education. Dr. Handy is the President/Chancellor/Founder of The New Testament Bible Church Biblical Institute. He serves as Professor of Theology and Practice of Ethics and Ministry. In April 2011, Dr. Handy was appointed **Bishop of the Louisiana Conference** from Fellowship of Christ International. His appointment was accredited to his many years of dedicated service to God, service to humanity, and ministry. His district covers the entire state of Louisiana.

ABOUT THE AUTHOR

His educational background includes studies in Business Administration from Louisiana Business College, a Bachelor's Degree in Religious Education, and a Bachelor's Degree in Theology, a Master's of Divinity Degree, and a Doctorate of Theology Degree from Andersonville Theological Seminary in Camilla, Ga. He has a Ph. D. in Philosophy in Counseling from the Institute of Christian Works in Columbia; SC. Dr. Handy is the Father of three children and definitely believes the family is the foundation of any society. Dr. Handy has received many citations and special recognition awards from many states and civic organizations across the US. Dr. Handy is a Louisiana State Certified Clinical Chaplain.

Other Books by Dr. Handy

*The Scars of Racism
*Readings For The Soul
*A Christian Guide To A New You
*Love Letters To My Future Bride and Wife To Be
*Help Lord, My Life Hurts
*What Does It Mean To Be A Christian?
*Saving Our Children
*Racism: The Absence of Good

Please Address Your Correspondence to:

Dr. Christopher D. Handy
P. O. Box 29578
Shreveport, LA. 71149
drcdhandy@gmail.com
http://icantbreathetoo.homestead.com